AURA AWARENESS

AURA AWARENESS
What Your Aura Says About You

Contributing Editors

C. E. LINDGREN, DLitt
JENNIFER BALTZ

Introduction By

GUY COGGINS
Inventor of the Aura Camera 6000
and *Interactive Biofeedback Field Imaging*

Aura Imaging — Progen Co.
1997

Cover art by Garret Moore
Interior drawings by Krystal Hipps

Publisher's Cataloging in Publication Data
(Prepared by Quality Books Inc.)

Aura awareness : what your aura says about you/
    C. E. Lindgren, Jennifer Baltz, editors.
    p. cm.
    Includes bibliographical references.
    ISBN: 0-9652490-5-0 (pbk.)
    1. Aura. 2. Chakras. 3. Kirlian photography.
    4. Self-actualization.   I. Lindgren, C. E. II. Baltz, Jennifer.
BF1389.A8B35 1996   133.8
QBI96-20425 Library of Congress No. 96-86093

FIRST EDITION
First Printing — 5000 — January 1997

Distributed to the trade by
Blue Dolphin Publishing, Inc.
P.O. Box 8, Nevada City, CA 95959
Orders: 1-800-643-0765

Printed in the United States of America

9   8   7   6   5   4   3   2   1

ACKNOWLEDGMENTS

Thanks to Dr. Buryl Payne, Guy Coggins, and Blythe Arakawa for their technical support, and in particular to the other contributors: Barbara Martin, Susana Madden, Janice Dye, and Ruby K. Corder. Thanks as well to those who agreed to have their photos printed. Also to Garret Moore for his cover design and to Krystal Hipps for her drawings. We couldn't have done it without you.

Our special thanks goes to all the authors and publishers for granting permission to reprint from their works. A partial listing includes:

Barbara Ann Brennan, *Hands of Light,* Bantam, New York, 1987.
Fate Magazine, published by Llewellyn Worldwide, Ltd.
Foundation for Inner Peace; "A Course in Miracles."
James Redfield, *The Celestine Prophecy,* Warner Books, 1993.
Patrick Allessandra, *Seeing Auras* (Internet publication).
Valerie V. Hunt, *Infinite Mind: The Science of Human Vibrations,*
    Malibu Publications, Malibu, CA, 1989.

Finally, our appreciation to the late V. Rt. Rev. Dr. Lewis S. Bostwick, founder of the Berkeley Psychic Institute and the other fine teachers in that organization.

TABLE OF CONTENTS

FOREWORD

Perceiving and Measuring the Human Aura

The aura has been seen for centuries, perhaps millenniums. Only a few times have I observed the aura of another person. One of the most dramatic times occurred when I guided a self-hypnotic session for a group of twelve people. Four of the twelve, including myself, clearly saw colored auras and agreed upon the colors we saw. The aura was bright and shimmery, rather like the light from a fluorescent tube, but not as intense. The colors were clearly visible in bright sunlight. This was a massage group. The four of us who saw colors noticed that when a person massaged someone, a colored patch appeared on the body. Different people produced colors of different hues on the person being massaged. After a few hours the ability to see the aura gradually went away. However, different people have different sensitivities. Whatever your natural ability to see an aura, you can probably enhance it with practice.

About the same time I saw auras, I also discovered a device which can detect, and even measure in numerical terms, a force around the body, which could be related to the aura that some people see all the time. (The colors of the aura are not measured by the device.) This force seems to be a rotational one, so that a frame suspended about the body will twist. The normal direction of twist is towards the right as seen from within, or clockwise as seen from above the head. The force is usually stronger at times of increased sunspot activity. At the time of a new or full moon, the direction of the rotation will temporarily reverse! This connection of the auric force around the body with the Sun's activity and Earth's magnetic activity adds another dimension to analysis of the human aura. We humans may be connected, by resonance, with the entire solar system.

Of course, a person's aura is not solely a function of the Earth's or Sun's activity: we do have our own input, our own energy force, which combines with the external forces to produce our resultant aura. For example, when a person is relaxed, meditating or feeling peaceful, the virtual spin force around the body is less. When a person is excited, stimulated, or fearful, the spin force increases. When a person has low energy, the spin force is reduced.

New tools in science have always led to new discoveries. There are so many interesting factors and aspects of the human aura to explore that one person, one small company, or even a well-funded research laboratory could not uncover them all. Everyone can participate in this field. Everybody's help is needed to fully advance our understanding of the human aura. Who knows what your own discoveries may trigger in the minds of others—leading them to carry it on.

Buryl Payne, PhD
Psychologist, Physicist, and Inventor
Santa Cruz, California

INTRODUCTION

The Hospital of the Future

I have always considered myself a dreamer, visionary, and creator. Perhaps my greatest dream is a world free of fear. Far too many individuals suffer needlessly. Therefore I am working for a future wherein science, technology, and human spirituality will merge for the betterment of all mankind.

Regarding this dream, I believe that hospitals in the future may employ a combination of modern surgical techniques and spiritual energy balancing, bringing together the best of both the ancient world and the present day. Say you injure your wrist playing tennis. As you enter the hospital, a spiritual counselor/nurse looks at your energy. The trained sensitive uses her intuition and her trained sense of touch to feel your wrist. The practitioner perceives your wrist with a little red here, some blue there. She waves her hand through your aura just around the wrist. Then she holds your wrist gently. You feel better. The nurse enters her observations into the computer: "It feels like a pulled ligament." She then sends you to the x-ray department to check for any fractures.

Then you go to the MRI, magnetic resonance imaging room. The MRI of the future may show not only the human body, but also could show the energy field around it in color displayed on a computer screen. Your future doctor watches the three-dimensional monitor and sees a pulled ligament surrounded by clouds of red. Your medical doctor applies a gentle osteopathic manipulation to soothe your wrist. After he is finished you notice that the monitor shows some cooler colors surrounding your wrist. Your doctor then wraps your wrist and prescribes medication and homeopathic medicines to reduce pain and induce healing. He also suggest talking with an intuitive counselor to discover the underlying spiritual cause of your injury.

With the counselor, you find that you subconsciously wanted the injury to happen because you would be able to take the day off from the stress and boredom of your job, which you hate. You finally decide to look for another job that is "more you," a position you can feel good about and enjoy.

In the future, a medical diagnostician may use color displayed as a field to make the information more understandable. At the present time, biofeedback Aura Imaging technology measures biological changes and depicts these values as an Aura. Aura Imaging is not approved or recommended for medical diagnosis or therapeutic purposes. The intended application is for the study of the human energy, relaxation, and spiritual development.

A New Way to See Human Energy

I became interested in the "New Age" movement through Kirlian photography. I discovered that an aura camera was developed in Russia in the 1930s that could photograph the energy—or corona discharge—of your fingertips and toes. I was practicing meditation and yoga at the time, too. My interest in auras was mystical, spiritual, and scientific. It seemed natural to me to blend together what I knew from each discipline. I built my first Kirlian-style aura camera in 1970.

I knew I could emit energy from my hands and wanted to prove it scientifically. I found I actually could make my Kirlian "fingertip photo" brighter at will. Just by concentrating, I could change the brightness of the "aura" around my fingertips! It was an exciting moment. I even thought I was divinely gifted—until some of my friends showed me how they could make their fingertip photos much brighter than mine! This was a lesson in spiritual humility.

To me, it just seemed like the most logical step to develop existing technology into a system that could show the energy field around someone's portrait. Aura imaging systems can help people see what is going on in their personal space, and seeing it is the first step towards making changes. As an inventor, my ideal is to make this technology so popular that everyone will learn to tell the truth. We all have impossible, unrealistic pictures we are supposed to live up to. These pictures come from the media, our families, friends, employers, relationships, and society in general. The more pressure there is to fulfill those impossible expectations, the more unconscious we become of them. As a result, we walk through much of life resisting what we "should" do and not seeing or having what we really *want*. If you can see those "shoulds" in your personal space, you can choose consciously how you want to deal with them. You can choose what you want in your life and create it.

This book is a tremendous first step. Play with it—like a kindergarten tool—to build your intuitive awareness and learn who you really are. When you begin expanding your intuitive awareness, you start to find your own truth. You blast through all the crazy illusions that held you prisoner without your even knowing it.

When we realize that everything originates from within, we'll see that all the love, peace, and happiness in the universe is inside, waiting to be expressed. That's when we'll discover pure joy. We can have that. It's really so simple and easy. When you learn about your aura, you can begin to see and appreciate the profound and unique splendor of your own energy.

The famous spiritual teacher and lecturer, Patricia Sun expressed it quite well in this prayer: *May we allow the energy of God to flow into us, vibrate within us, expand out and radiate from us— as us.*

As you become aware of your aura and the energy of other living beings and situations around you, you can go beyond the unconscious. You enter into a new reality of awareness and make better choices in your life.

Guy Coggins, President
PROGEN COMPANY
Inventor of the Aura Camera 3000 & 6000
and Interactive Biofeedback Field Imaging

WE ARE MADE OF LIGHT

-1-

Jennifer Baltz

You are a child of the universe, no less than the trees and the stars; you have a right to be here. And whether or not it is clear to you, no doubt the universe is unfolding as it should.

Max Ehrmann, *Desiderata* (1692)

What is an Aura, Anyway?

"He is really shining brightly today." "You're lit up like a Christmas tree!" "She glowed with expectation." "He has such positive energy." "She just radiates joy." Have you ever used these kinds of words to describe someone? Has anyone used these words to talk about you? When people use this kind of language, what they are really doing is describing your *energy field*—your *aura.*

The aura is an energy field that radiates through and around all living things. Scientists, psychics, and spiritual teachers have all perceived auras in various ways. We humans have auras. So do animals—and even plants. Author and teacher Barbara Brennan (1987, 5), a former atmospheric physicist with NASA, talks about seeing the aura of trees as a child in her book *Hands of Light:*

> When I practiced walking blindfolded in the woods, I would feel the trees long before I could touch them with my hands. I realized the trees were larger than they appeared to the visual eye. Trees have life energy fields around them, and I was sensing those fields.

As she played and explored the world around her, Brennan developed her ability to actually see energy—to see the aura: "Later I learned to see the energy fields of trees and the small animals. I discovered that everything has an energy field around it that looks somewhat like the light from a candle" (Brennan 1987, 5).

Why Should You Learn More About Auras?

Your aura is an extension of who you are. To a clairvoyant, your aura speaks volumes about where you have been, what you are creating in your life, and where you are going. It shows your personality, how you relate to other people, and how you treat yourself.

Your actions, thoughts, and emotions can show up in your aura. By becoming more aware of your aura, you can learn about yourself and grow in ways that most people cannot even imagine.

Suppose for a moment that you are having trouble getting over a broken relationship. Everywhere you go, you cannot help but think about that person. You see him or her in your dreams—in fact you see that person every time you close your eyes to relax. You cannot help wondering what if, what might have been. You experience tremendous grief and loss.

When you have more awareness of the energy around you, you might realize that those continual mental images of your former beloved are in fact bits of his or her energy still stuck in your personal space—your aura. Perhaps that person still has attention focused on you, and you are feeling it. Energetic cords of communication are still connected between you. This is what I usually find when I do readings on this topic, by the way. When you understand that most of that grief and loss is actually the energy and attention of the other person, you can take a giant step in letting him or her go and getting on with your life in happiness and joy.

Finding Your Own Path

Becoming more aware of energy means that you can tell when a particular path is right for you. Say, for example, you are offered two jobs. Company #1 pays less, but it seems brighter somehow. You like the people there, and they seem like they are having fun. Company #2 has a more prestigious position. It pays a lot more and has great benefits, but you get the feeling that it isn't as friendly an atmosphere. People seem a little more stressed. Which do you choose? Many of us would choose the higher paying, more prestigious position and simply ignore those nagging little intuitions that something isn't quite right with that company.

But what if you tuned in a little more and felt the energy of the people around you? You'd see that the auras of the employees at Company #1 really resonate with your energy. You would feel a real kinship with them. Also, you might notice from the brightness and strength of their auras that huge success is just around the corner for that company. Looking more closely at Company #2, you discover that the supervisor is hiding something. How? Because you can see his aura shake with uncertainty every time he talks about the company's glowing future. You can also see the gray, unhappy energy in the auras of the employees. Now which company would you choose?

"That's all well and good," you might be thinking, "but I could never sense an aura. I could never feel energy like that." Not so. Your aura is part of you, as you will soon see. You have the capability to learn more about it, to understand it, and to sense it and the energy fields of others, too. That ability is innate—it is inside you. You may find that you are better at feeling energy than seeing it, or vice versa. Or, you may find that you just "know" something. That is fine, too. For each of us, intuitive abilities manifest differently.

As you read this book, allow yourself to notice what you feel, what you experience. Be open to the possibility that you can sense the world on a deeper level. You may find yourself experiencing strange coincidences, or getting flashes of awareness—especially in doing the exercises at the end of the book.

One of the biggest reasons why more people are not "psychic" is that they don't give themselves permission to be more aware. They close the doorways to their intuition because subconsciously they feel it is wrong or dangerous. These beliefs can be ingrained deeply from childhood. So, be patient with yourself. Give yourself permission to look at life in a new way.

In this book, we'll show you how to start sensing the aura. Finally, you'll learn about the colors and energies in your aura and what they say about you.

WHAT YOUR AURA LOOKS LIKE

-2-

Jennifer Baltz

"The whole of Einstein's life's work was to show that what we perceive as hard matter is mostly empty space with a pattern of energy running through it. This includes ourselves."

James Redfield, *The Celestine Prophecy*

Your Personal Universe

Imagine a space filled with radiant light. Energy flows and swirls through it in bright colors. This *life energy* moves around you as you sit nestled safely in the center. This place is your aura: your own personal universe. It is your protection and your playground. It constantly moves and changes as you move and change.

Auras come in every color of the rainbow. As a psychic, I have found that the human aura consists of seven layers, or levels (figure 1: Aura Man). The colors and energies in your aura can change in a short period of time, although you may have a basic color, or combination of colors, that stays constant. These colors are your signature. Think of them as your "favorite colors." These colors are part of your personality—they make you an individual because they reflect your life experience.

The basic colors in your aura can evolve over time, just as you do. Gina Allan (1996), a Naturopath, former Buddhist nun, and best-selling author of *Gifts of Spirit,* says that her aura colors have changed over time with her own personal growth: "Over the last

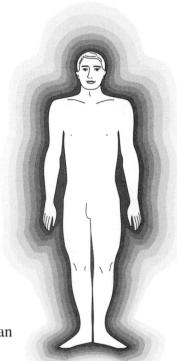

Figure 1: Aura Man

fifteen years, I have been observing changes taking place in the spiritual colours of my own aura. I have had these colours confirmed by a friend who sees auras. . . . Fifty years ago my colours showed a very pale aqua green, indicating clairvoyant abilities. Today that colour is a deep sea green when I'm doing energy work or speaking on the subject." For Allan, the deeper green color reflects her increased certainty and ability. It shows her spiritual evolution.

Auras are flexible—in other words, *they change all of the time*. Size, colors, texture, and density can all change depending on your state of mind and what you are experiencing in life. Usually, though, there is a basic pattern that we use as a "default." For example, UCLA researcher Dr. Valerie Hunt (1989, 75) noticed that women tend to carry more energy around their upper bodies, and men often have bigger auras around the lower half of their bodies. As a clairvoyant, I often notice that people who think a lot about the future push their auras farther out in front. People who spend a lot of time remembering the past, or who don't want to plan for the future, often have more energy behind them.

The size and shape of your aura is unique to you. Your aura could be bigger in front of you than it is behind. Some auras come to a "point" at the top, while others are more egg-shaped. There are really no "typical" auras, because we are all different. Your aura can extend out a few inches from your skin, or many feet. Some people have auras that are as big as a house!

People with small auras, for example, tend to "fade into the woodwork" at parties and in other social situations. They pull their auras close to their bodies so that they won't be noticed! People with big auras can dominate a room and look powerful—or feel overbearing, depending on your point of view.

Seeing the Aura Through Time

Almost every culture on Earth acknowledges the existence of the human aura (or energy field) in some form. Chinese medicine dates back thousands of years. Its focus is the flow of ch'i, or energy, through and around the body. Yoga, East Indian religious beliefs, and even Tantric lovemaking practices are all based on the human energy system of aura and chakras. Spiritualism as practiced in Brazil, the Philippines, and other countries is also based on the fact that we are made of flowing energy as well as matter. Most of these practices have a core belief that when energy is manipulated and changed, it can lead to changes in the physical body.

Artists have painted the aura for centuries. It is usually associated with royalty or religious figures. From the very beginnings of Christianity, religious art has depicted Jesus, Mary, and the saints with auras. In the painting on the next page, notice that the Virgin Mary is shown with light coming from her body, as well as a halo of light around her head. The light rays around her body are called the nimbus, or "radiant luminescence," and the halo is called an aureole. Both are part of her aura.

The Virgin in Glory, Italy, 14th Century, Anonymous.
The Vatican, courtesy Alimar/Art Resource

Nostradamus—Visionary and Seer of Auras

One of my favorite "aura stories" is one I heard from famous psychic Dayle Schear (1996). This story is about Michel de Nostradame, also known as Nostradamus. Born in 1503, Nostradamus was an extraordinary psychic. In his day, he was most noted as a respected doctor who saved the lives of many plague victims. Today we remember him for his surprisingly accurate predictions.

Nostradamus wrote his visions in poetic verse so that he would not be burned as a heretic in an age when anyone with unusual abilities was at risk from the Inquisition. Despite his stature, Nostradamus was not immune from the witch trials—the protection of Queen Catherine de Medici once saved him from death by burning!

One day, Nostradamus was traveling down a narrow road and chanced to meet a group of Franciscan monks. He stepped aside for them to pass—and noticed one monk in particular. This man's golden aura was so overwhelmingly beautiful that it brought Nostradamus to tears. As Brother Felice Peretti passed by, the doctor fell to his knees in the mud and gave homage to him.

The other monks were puzzled, since young Brother Peretti was the lowly son of a swine herder. Nostradamus replied that he must bow to his Holiness. The monks laughed and went on their way, no doubt telling the story about the crazy doctor and teasing young Peretti about it for years.

Forty years later, Brother Felice Peretti became His Holiness, Pope Sixtus V. Nostradamus did not live to see his prediction come true, however—he died twenty years before Peretti donned his papal robes (Schear 1996).

Quantum Reality

You don't have to be a psychic to see an aura—and you certainly don't have to be a saint to have one. Over the past 100 years, scientists have been discovering what mystics and clairvoyants have known from the beginning of time: living creatures radiate energy. Every living thing on our planet gives off life energy. This energy can be measured with instruments, and now it can even be represented on film, as you see with the aura pictures in this book.

Scientists used to think that we were made of matter and that matter was solidly composed of particles. Now, they are discovering through quantum physics that we are really made of *energy fields* instead. Gary Zukov's *The Dancing Wu Li Masters* is a highly readable and understandable exploration of quantum mechanics if you would like to learn more about this subject.

Dr. Valerie Hunt, a professor and researcher at UCLA has studied the aura for more than 20 years. In her book, *Infinite Mind: The Science of Human Vibrations,* Dr. Hunt (1989, 48) concludes: "As a result of my work, I can no longer consider the body as organic systems or tissues. The body is a flowing, interactive electrodynamic energy field."

In other words, we are made of energy and space. The energy making up the human body is dense enough to see and touch. It feels solid. The aura is a little "lighter," less dense, and not so easy to see with the physical eyes. Almost anyone can feel the energy of the aura with their hands, however. It just takes a little practice.

"Let Me Balance Your Aura"

My first "aura encounter" happened at Santa Clara University, a very conservative Jesuit college in Northern California. A bright, vivacious English teacher burst into the grants office where I worked part-time and offered to give me an "aura balancing." She was taking a meditation class, and she needed to "clean out" my aura as homework!

Now, I am an engineer's daughter. I was raised on science and skepticism in the heart of Silicon Valley. The scientific part of me was positive she had gone off the deep end. But something inside me was enchanted with her enthusiasm, so I agreed. She waved her hands around my head and body, closing "holes" in my aura. The funny part about it was that I could actually feel her hands moving around me even when I had my eyes closed. Much to my surprise, I felt more centered and energized after she finished.

A few years later after my encounter in college, I walked into the Berkeley Psychic Institute in Northern California and noticed similar hand-waving activity. Within a few weeks, I learned how to feel an aura with my hands. With that experience, my concept of life changed forever. I began walking down an ever-changing road of growth and expanding awareness, starting in the Institute's clairvoyant training program. I learned to use psychic abilities like clairvoyance, telepathy, and clairsentience. I also discovered that I was *already using* most of these abilities without realizing it. You may be, too.

Although they are rather exotic-sounding, psychic gifts are not that different from abilities like playing the piano or swimming. As I mentioned in the first chapter, all human beings have the ability to feel energy—it's part of having a human body. It's just a matter of becoming more conscious of what is around you. Like most skills, the more you practice, the better you become at it. You might find that one skill is easier for you than another—for instance, you might be better at clairsentience (feeling the emotions of another person) than clairvoyance (clear-seeing).

Sensing Energy

Have you ever felt as though someone "took a bite out of you" in an argument? I remember an occasion when a co-worker came to me and complained that every time she spoke with Stacy (who worked in my department) she felt like she'd been attacked by a shark! And she was accurate in that feeling. Stacy was very good at taking "energy bites" out of people's auras when she did not get her way. She was angry about her life and felt that people owed her something. So, she simply took what she needed—namely a chunk of their life force energy. People would walk away with large holes in their auras after a confrontation with her. Are there any Stacys in *your* life?

You also might notice that certain people just seem brighter than others. Something about them sparkles. It is usually because they have more life energy in their bodies—their auras are bigger and clearer than average. When I see this, it usually means that the individual is happy, and doing what he or she was born to do. It also tells me that the person probably takes good care of his or her body, too.

When you fall in love, that warm fuzzy feeling you get is the blending of your aura with your beloved's aura. You might notice that even when you are apart from each other, it seems like you can still feel your partner's energy, or even see his or her face in your mind when you close your eyes. A friend of mine once woke up certain that her mate was lying in bed next to her—she said she could actually *feel* his body warmth—only to remember that he was really out of town on a business trip! Have you ever had this sensation?

Good Vibrations

In the 1960s, people talked about "vibes." You either had good vibes or bad ones, but you definitely had them! The word "vibes" really refers to your energy, to your aura. You might not actually see auras with your physical eyes (yet!), but you do feel energy. We all sense energy on a subconscious level every day.

This is why two people who look and dress similarly will often be perceived as totally different. It's because their energy *is* different. When you meet someone for the first time, that "first impression" you get is a combination of physical characteristics and the energy in his or her *aura*.

For instance, you walk into a car dealership, looking to buy a new car. Two salesmen are on the lot, and you happen to see *them* before they see *you* (I know, it's unlikely, but bear with me for a minute!). Both of these guys are dressed in blue suits with power red ties. They both have brown hair. But as you watch them, you get the feeling that the one on the left is more down-to-earth, a little easier to work with than the other guy. And he's the one you go to see. What you're doing is actually sensing the salesman's energy, or auric field, and making a decision based on what you notice!

Why You Have an Aura

Your aura consists of life force energy. You, as an immortal spirit, are the breath of life that animates your body. Indeed, the word "spirit" comes from *spiritus*, which means "breath" in Latin. Your aura is an extension of you as spirit and body. Often strong emotions or other life events will show themselves in your aura before you experience them in physical reality. In his essay, *Auras*, Edgar Cayce mentions a friend of his who wore almost nothing but blue for most of his life. Blue was the main color in his aura as well. Suddenly, he began selecting maroon and red accessories like ties and handkerchief sets. Cayce noted that the red energy had begun to appear quite strongly in his aura. He also became more nervous and began working too hard. (Too much red may lead to over-stimulation and anxiety.) Eventually, this man became very tired. During the course of the exhaustion, his aura was very gray. Then, he began to regain his energy as his natural blue colors asserted themselves once again (Cayce 1945, 10).

Body, mind, aura, spirit—all of these parts make up the whole that is you. An imbalance in any part can create dysfunction in the whole. It's important to note where the problem started so that you can remedy it. Many problems we have are based on emotional issues. Louise Hay's book *You Can Heal Your Life* is an excellent resource for learning more about why you have created certain problems in your life. By clearing the original cause, you reduce the chance of repeating that particular pattern in the future.

A vibrant aura can act as a protective field for your personal space (BPI 1989). When the aura is charged up and bright with vital energy, personal troubles tend to "slide" right off of it. Do you remember when Ronald Reagan was dubbed the "Teflon®-coated President"? Nothing stuck to him. Why? It was probably a combination of his loyal White House staff and his industrial-strength aura!

We tend to forget our own no-stick days, although we all have them. There are times when no one can get you down. No matter what happens, no matter what anyone says, you're having fun and life is grand. These are the times when your aura is bright, expansive, and flowing smoothly. This is your natural state of energy balance. When the energy in your aura stops moving, or gets muddy or damaged through stress from an encounter with someone like Stacy (or perhaps even your mother), your protection is weakened. You can become tired, or just plain energy depleted when your aura is stuck or torn. This is where awareness comes in. When you stop and "check in" with your aura, you can get a feel for how vibrant it is. See the chapter of aura exercises near the end of this book for ways to do this.

Aura Experiments

Plants have auras, too, as many scientists have discovered. Their auras are also subject to damage and low vitality when they experience trauma. In her book, *The Probability of the Impossible*, Dr. Thelma Moss (1974, 45-49) discusses experiments with the life force energy of plants. She photographed leaves with Kirlian photography, a technique developed in Russia in the 1930s that shows the aura, or energy field, around leaves, fingertips, and small objects. The first photograph, of a leaf just picked off a plant, shows vibrant energy radiating through and around the leaf. The same cut leaf, three days later, showed less life-force energy because it was not receiving any nourishment from the mother plant. Fifteen days later, the leaf was virtually dead, with little or no life-force energy running through it.

On the flip side, positive emotions can lead to more energy in the aura—as you can see from the Kirlian image of fingertips (page 25). The top fingertip is of a man in a relaxed state. The bottom fingertip was photographed while the same man was thinking of his girlfriend. The darker spots in the center of the bottom fingertip photo are actually reds and oranges—colors of vitality and passion that sparked at the thought of his lady!

Manifesting Your Dreams Through Your Aura

Your aura is also your playground. It is your personal universe, where you begin to manifest what you want (BPI 1989). Many people look outward for the things they want in life—thinking that someone else can help them get what they want. But the truth is that everything in your life is generated first within your aura. You can't create it out there "in the real world" unless you create space for it *inside yourself* first.

That's a pretty bold statement to make, but time and time again in psychic readings, I have found it to be true. A couple who believe their business will fail creates mental "pictures" of failing and put those pictures in their respective auras. Sooner or later, those pictures become real, and their business does indeed go under.

Mental pictures are simply the images you see in your mind when you think about a particular person, place, or thing. They can be memories, desires for the future, telepathic thoughts picked up from someone else, or from a particular object (BPI 1989). I often experience these images when visiting old houses or museums. Once, I visited the Asian Art Museum in San Francisco to look at an exhibit of antique Turkish rugs. As I walked through the carpets, I could see in my mind's eye the images of people sitting on the carpets eating dinner, talking, fighting. I was seeing the afterimages, or energy patterns still left on the rugs from their previous owners. This, incidentally, is how a clairvoyant "sees."

Mental pictures can be created in your head and then transferred to the energy field around your body—your aura. If you create a picture that you are a little too fat in the rear end, you will invariably take that picture and place it right on your posterior. Then, each time you look in the mirror, you subconsciously see the picture and reinforce that negative image: "See, I knew I was too fat." This is one reason why so many people end up gaining weight while on a diet—the negative image pictures they create about themselves get reinforced so much that it is hard to break them.

You can also collect pictures given to you by other people. Say your boss says that you did a great job on a project. She creates a mental picture that you are doing well and gives it to you along with the words "Good job!" You take that picture, put it into your aura, and refer to it the next time you have a similar project to do. "I can do this," you reason. And you have her picture right there to back you up.

We tend to store images of both positive validation and negative criticism in our auras, much like we gather clutter in our houses. Think about it. If you wake up every day to a mess, then you may find yourself subconsciously creating more messes in your life as a result. You might find that your energy feels cluttered and stuck simply because your house is filled with clutter.

Since you live in your aura all the time (think of it as a second skin, or a favorite t-shirt), you live in the middle of those pictures you generate or collect from other people. It follows that whatever images and energy you bring into your aura are the things you will begin to manifest in real life. You can't help but do so since you "see" them all the time in your space. When you focus on something constantly, you give it life; you give it substance.

Bringing in images of what you want to create and storing them in your aura will give you both a reference point and a doorway for those things to enter your life. A woman who knows that she can and will have true love in her life will invariably find it, because she puts the image of what she wants in the outermost edge of her aura. The certainty and desire in the picture acts like a magnet to attract Mr. Right.

It's like the story of two men who went on vacation at the same five-star resort. Both men had identical suites. Both pursued the same activities; both ate the same seven-course buffet dinners. One man totally loved his vacation. The other hated it and complained to the resort about bad service.

The only difference between the two men was the attitude they projected before and during their trips. The first man, who enjoyed himself immensely, went there with a positive attitude. He knew he was going to have fun, and he constantly projected a fun attitude during his trip. The second man went reluctantly. He couldn't relax, thinking of the piles of work that were waiting for him back at the office. He decided at the outset that the vacation was a waste of time. He set out to prove himself right by projecting that thought into his vacation.

We project our thoughts, or mental image "pictures," out into the world, just as the two men did. Our external reality is created based on those projections. If your aura contains the energy "picture" that other people are usually mean, then that is what you will draw to you. If your aura contains the thought that people are basically nice, you will tend to bring out the best in those around you.

In his book, *Creating Affluence: Wealth Consciousness in the Field of All Possibilities*, Deepak Chopra M.D. (1993, 28) talks about the flow of energy in our universe—that "field of all possibilities." He redefines the Golden Rule of "Do unto others as you would have them do unto you." In essence, he says that when you express particular attitudes, they come back to you. Like attracts like. Act in abundance and you will receive even more abundance in return. *A Course in Miracles* (Foundation n.d., 445) says the same thing in a different way: "Projection makes perception. The world you see is what you gave it, nothing more than that. But though it is no more than that, it is not less. Therefore, to you it is important. It is the witness to your state of mind, the outside picture of an inward reality." So, when you express a positive attitude, it begins to "stick" in your aura. That positive energy in your aura attracts positive events into your life.

The Structure of the Aura

Working as a psychic, I have found that the aura consists of seven major levels, or layers of energy. The first three layers relate to the body—issues about food, shelter, money, relationships, how much energy you have for daily activities, and so forth. The middle, or fourth, layer connects spirit and human body, and relates specifically to affinity—love for yourself and others. The outer three layers are related to your spiritual essence. They reflect your ability to communicate, imagine, see clairvoyantly, and bring your core essence as a spirit into your physical body (BPI 1989).

All the layers work together. Energy moves from layer to layer, and often spreads throughout the layers. The aura constantly moves, spinning clockwise. Dr. Buryl Payne claims to have actually demonstrated this with a patented instrument which measures the aura's torque, or spin!

The Physical Aura

The first three layers of your aura closest to the body are often called the physical aura since they relate to body matters. These levels of energy are what the hero in *The Celestine Prophecy* began to see around plants and people as he discovered the Third Insight (Redfield 1993).

The **first layer** of the aura (also known as the **etheric layer**) is seen closest to the skin. It relates to survival issues like food, water, shelter and work, as well as physical needs or desires. In a vital, happy person, it is often a bright strong color. In a person who does not have much energy, the color might be more subdued, grayish, or even darkened. If you are pretty good at manifesting your basic needs in life—food, shelter, clothing and so forth—the first layer of your aura is usually in good shape.

The **second, or emotional, layer** of the aura has to do with the emotional state and relationships with other people. This is the layer where the body expresses and stores emotions—in a reading, this is often where I look to see what emotions a person is feeling or repressing. The repressed emotions look darker and more constricted. Happiness, sadness, anger, joy—all of these can be seen in the second layer of your aura. In readings, I often see that people take on the problems of their family or friends and put them in this part of the aura. If you find yourself feeling sad after comforting an unhappy friend, you might be taking on his/her sadness as your own!

The **third, or mental, layer** focuses on the mind-body connection, and the feeding of life force energy throughout the body. A weakened or thinning layer here means that the individual may not have the energy or willpower to follow through on his or her goals. A strong third layer indicates that these thoughts and actions are in harmony. In other words, while the first layer reflects everyday survival issues, this layer shows how much you are enjoying your day-to-day activities, and how much energy there is to carry them out.

The **fourth (astral) layer** of the aura is of the heart—here are issues of love, connection, affinity, and oneness. This is both a link between the body, mind, and spirit, and a connection with all other people and living creatures on Planet Earth. A large, brightly-colored fourth layer can indicate a person who values human connections and puts his or her relationships above all else in life.

The **fifth layer** of the aura, also known as the **etheric template,** is a place of communication and creative expression. Often, if this layer is blocked or dark, the person has probably been feeling isolated from the world. A strong fifth layer indicates someone who communicates well with others, often through creative talents such as writing, teaching, public speaking, art or music.

The **sixth, or celestial, layer** of the aura represents the visual senses. It also shows how you see the world—those attitudes and images that you manifest into reality are often located here. Your intuitive abilities are often seen here as well. Someone with a strong sixth layer, or who shows a clear indigo blue in this layer, often is a person who sees the truth plainly.

The **seventh, or ketheric, layer** of the aura is the outer edge: the layer that other people see when they look at you. Here, are often held mental images of who you are and who you want to be. Many times, people put a "shield" of energy here so that others cannot see their innermost selves. Shields like this can be quite effective at screening out other people, but they also can have the effect of hiding you from the people you *want* to connect with. When the seventh layer is shining brightly, it shows a person who is unafraid of the judgments and criticisms of others. Spiritual masters often have bright seventh layers. So do people who are following their hearts' desire and are not afraid to let their light shine in whatever they choose to undertake.

Once again, every aura is different: it reflects the energy and personality of its owner. Almost any question you have can be answered by looking in this personal universe called your aura— not only from *this* lifetime but also from every *past life* you've ever lived.

SCIENCE MEETS THE UNKNOWN
Early Adventures with the Human Aura

-3-

C. E. Lindgren, DLitt

Acceptance of our expansiveness beyond the known reality of the self, is release of the ego. Ego can only perceive from a three dimensional viewpoint, with a concept of "I exist, as I believe I exist." Auric vision is a threat to the ego's concept of self (existing only within the physical form) and, therefore, cannot be achieved unless fear of the unknown is abandoned through the release of concept of self.

Janice Dye, Reiki Practitioner

The aura has been known by many names over the centuries—ch'i, prana, karnaeem, and Illiaster. In fact, it has been documented for over 5,000 years. Astral lights alluded to by ancient Eastern Indians, Chinese and Jewish mystics are attributed to a universal energy that permeates all matter. The aura has been described in early esoteric writings and later in those of the Rosicrucians, Zen Buddhists, Christian mystics—even in the oral traditions of the American Indians. Many writings strongly suggest that the auric field intensity correlates to Chinese acupuncture energy meridians.

According to some, the ability to see auras is part of man's evolutionary development—in time we will all be able to do so! This theory is advanced in Steve Richards' book, *Invisibility: Mastering the Art of Vanishing*. Patrick Alessandra, author of *Seeing Auras*, says that

In the last decade of the twentieth century, there are far more people alive than ever before who can not only feel but also see the energies around them. This is a natural event in human evolution and as more years pass we will all find our ability to sense auras and energies increasing.

To see where we are headed, it helps to take a look at the recent past—science's early attempts to document the human aura.

Dr. Walter Kilner

In 1869, Walter Kilner joined the student body of London's St. Thomas's Hospital and began researching "electrotherapy." Ten short years later, he was appointed in charge of the hospital's electro-therapy department (Shepard 1965, vi). By 1897, the first X-ray department in London was established at St. Thomas' Hospital—and Dr. Kilner was placed in charge. Kilner paid special attention to the works and writings of other progressive thinkers as well. Baron Carl von Reichenbach was one of the first to publish articles on the "odic force," or human aura. American Dr. Edwin Babbitt continued with a prodigious study of how color affected the human electromagnetic field (Ferguson 1973).

Kilner was also aware of clairvoyants and mediums of the day who spoke of the auric field, and he had read the illustrated writings of C. W. Leadbeater on the aura. Dr. Kilner decided to study the human energy field, and he began tinkering with devices to make the aura visible to the naked eye. Through a series of objective and subjective experiments, Dr. Kilner invented a detection device to observe the human aura.

His device hinged on a blue dye called dicyanin. When looking through a glass lens colored with this dye, Dr. Kilner and his colleagues discovered that they could see vaporous energy (auras) extending from living bodies (Kilner 1965, 4). Dr. Kilner discovered that the longer he looked through the blue lens, the more sensitive his own eyes became to ultraviolet and higher light spectrums. In his 1911 book, *The Human Atmosphere* (later reissued in 1965 as *The Human Aura*), Dr. Kilner claimed to present scientific evidence for the existence of the human aura. According to Kilner's research, he and his associates were able to see auric energy extending several inches from the patient's naked body: "After a few minutes we were surprised to find that we could continue to see the Aura without the intervention of the screen. This power did not last long. However, it was renewed by looking at the light for a few seconds through a dark screen" (Kilner 1973, 6-7).

Dr. Kilner made detailed observations of what he noticed. In particular, he noticed differences in male and female auras, and in the auras of young children. In general, he noted that women had more energy around their pelvic area—especially women of child-bearing years (Kilner 1973, Ch. 1). Given that extra energy is needed to create children, his observations make sense!

What Kilner and others who followed him were looking at was the physical aura, the first few layers of the aura. They saw this energy usually between two and five inches out around the body. Sometimes they also noticed a more vaporous cloud of energy farther out—what Kilner calls the "outer aura." This was most likely the outer, more spiritual layers of the human aura.

Dr. Kilner's work met with skepticism in the medical community. It was not until after he died in 1920 that a favorable review of his book appeared in the *Medical Times*. Later, Oscar Bagnall, a young man who continued Kilner's work, expanded on his theories in *The Origin and Properties of the Human Aura* (1937).

The Adventure Continues: Oscar Bagnall

Bagnall began his work by studying color blindness, then became curious about Dr. Kilner's research. He expanded on Kilner's theory, using a simpler method and a less dangerous dye (dicyanin caused blindness and burning on contact.) It was Bagnall's belief that the aura colors seen by the naked eye were subjective: in other words, they change from person to person. But he also believed that the aura itself "is objective fact." Bagnall

(1970, 31 & 40) thought that the aura was made of light rays shorter than the visible spectrum: ultraviolet light.

Nikola Tesla

For over 100 years, researchers have tried to photograph the aura. Nikola Tesla is regarded by many as the brightest inventor of all time. The father of modern electrical power. Tesla was working with alternating current at a time when Thomas Edison had no understanding of it. His Tesla coil is the heart of early radio transmitters. Tesla technology is the basis of Kirlian photography. In the 1890s, Tesla succeeded in taking the first aura photograph. He took photos not only of the auras around finger tips, but also of entire body auras, using a device that was attached to the body of his subject.

The Kirlian Experiment

Shortly after Bagnall's experiments, a radically new visual technique for auric detection was created. Soviet scientists Semyon and Valentina Kirlian (c. 1939) developed a method for photographing and viewing the aura. It was much more practical than the device developed by Nikola Tesla, which involved attaching the human subject to the device with electrical wires. Kirlian photography creates an image of the energy around a living form. You've probably seen photos of fingertips and leaves taken with a Kirlian camera (note Kirlian photo).

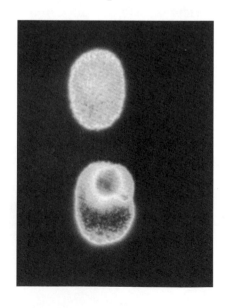

The technique involves using electric current to expose the presence of energy patterns—which are then transferred to a photographic plate.

The subject places his fingertip on the condensor-like plate. As overhead lights are turned down, a ghostly blue light rises from the plate area and a strong odor of ozone fills the air. The pad produces a crackling sound as high voltage (low amperage) electrical current is transferred from the plate to the subject's fingertip. Once the photo is developed, the print shows an array of brightly colored lights extending from the fingertip.

With this technique, the Kirlians, and later V. M. Inyushin and Victor Ademenko, also of the Soviet Union, studied the life force of leaves, seeds, fingertips, and the effect of psychic energy on plants. In one photo of a psychic's finger, the center of the fingertip was dark, with brilliant blue, red, and orange light surrounding it.

According to Stan Krippner and Daniel Rubin (1972) in *Galaxies of Life*, researchers were divided in their evaluation of the Kirlian phenomena. Some called the manifestation "corona discharge" and believed that the technique only reveals commonplace electrical occurrences. Others believed that radiation field photography reveals the *bioplasma body*, or aura.

WHERE TECHNOLOGY AND ENERGY MEET
The Aura Goes High Tech

-4-

C. E. Lindgren, DLitt

It was the first time for me. I sat on a stool in Linda's studio, placed my hands on metal boxes with sensors, and faced the camera. Linda switched on the power source and computerized camera. Everything was still and silent a few moments, and we were done.

George Liles, staff writer, *Provincetown Banner*

Kirlian Photography Heads West:
Dr. Thelma Moss

In the early 1970s, the auric investigations that started years earlier with the Kirlians in Russia began to migrate to the West. The Psychical Research Foundation and Department of Electrical Engineering at Duke University began investigating not only Kirlian photography but also a technique known as biolumines-cence. This procedure used highly sensitive light amplifiers to map faint natural light that allegedly radiated from some living organisms. Kirlian photography, however, possessed a near-magical quality which continued to draw researchers.

On the West Coast at UCLA, Dr. Thelma Moss began her research with Kirlian photography. In her book, *The Probability of the Impossible*, Dr. Moss (1974) talks about explorations of the human energy field. She notes that in her research, she could not find a correlation between skin temperature or moisture and the changes in the energy field on Kirlian fingertip photos.

Many scientists at the time believed that the variations in color, shape, and size of the aura on film were really due to variables like moisture, salt content, and gases produced by the skin. However, these explanations did not account for the so-called "phantom-leaf" effect wherein a portion of a leaf is removed and a Kirlian print is made showing energy outlining the missing portion of the leaf. These effects were first noted by Soviet scientists and later confirmed by Dr. Moss.

Lois Julien (1996), one of Dr. Moss' assistants at the lab, says "We wanted to make sure that we were on the right track. We did all sorts of tests to make sure that it wasn't something else like sweat. We studied the effects of moisture, temperature, the room, the atmosphere, the film. We eliminated all of these factors. What it came down to was energy."

In other words, Kirlian photos supposedly measure the energy field around your body. Once she established this fact, Dr. Moss and her volunteers began various studies using the Kirlian photos.

One test involved how the aura reacted in relationships. Julien relates the story of one young girl, sent to the lab by UCLA's psychology department. "The psych department sent us some teenagers in therapy with their parents. One girl came in and she and I put our fingertips down on the film (to take a Kirlian photo). We both had nice wide emanations of energy around our fingertips. Then I left the room and her parents came in. The resulting photo showed that the girl's aura got smaller around her fingertip, and the parents' had nice large energy fields." Being around her parents caused the girl to reduce the size of her aura—to shrink inward! "This was very consistent from family to family," notes Julien (1996). "They went back to therapy and discussed it—the photo became a jumping-off point to discuss the issue."

Dr. Moss also studied *energy transference* between people. Julien describes one experiment: "I tend to have quite an energetic outgoing personality. One day, Dr. Moss said, 'Lois, you are so bubbly today. I'd love to have some of that energy.' One of her assistants got an idea: 'Why don't you two go in and see if Lois can transfer her energy to Thelma?' So we tried it. At first, my fingertip photo had little tiny bubbles all round it, and hers didn't. We both concentrated on my transferring energy to her. In the second picture, bubbles from my fingertip went over to hers and surrounded her fingertip!"

Dr. Moss (1974, 45-49) also did "green thumb" and "brown thumb" experiments. People with "green thumbs" held a damaged leaf in their hands and focused on "repairing" the leaf. Before and after photos were taken of the leaf, and of a "control" leaf that was not touched. She even tried "sending energy at a distance," where the sender simply focused his thoughts on the leaf in question without touching it. What she found was that the "repaired" leaves had a brighter aura than the other leaves. She also discovered that many of the people who volunteered as "brown thumbs," (aka plant killers) really were—the plants actually responded negatively to their touch!

Bringing Aura Research into the Mainstream:
Dr. Valerie Hunt

Valerie Hunt began studying the aura at the University of California in Los Angeles. Her Energy Fields Laboratory has hosted studies with clairvoyants, dancers, patients with physical or mental problems, and many more volunteers. Dr. Hunt devised a technique wherein standard EMG electrodes were used to detect changes in bioelectrical energy on portions of the skin located over the chakra points. Dr. Hunt found that color changes in the aura observed by psychics correspond with the EMG recordings. Aura colors were associated with different observed wave patterns registered at the chakra points. In this way, Dr. Hunt showed that the chakras and aura work together in the human energy field. Dr. Hunt (1989, 33) measured the energy frequencies and amplitudes in chakras before, during, and after Rolfing (bodywork) sessions:

From approximately 600 hours of recording under many circum-
stances, we discovered that each person has a unique, predictable
and recurring field characterized by such measures as color, the
quantity of energy, the dominance of particular body areas, and the
completeness of the spectrum pattern. . . . Individual fields showed
areas where energy flowed more freely while others were blocked.

According to Dr. Hunt (1989, 33), the human energy field, or
aura, changes before the physical body does. "We discovered by
recording brain waves, blood pressure changes, galvanic skin
responses, heartbeat and muscle contraction simultaneously with
auric changes, that changes occurred in the field before any of the
other systems changed."

Aura Science: Barbara Ann Brennan

This research has profound implications for psychic energy
work. Barbara Ann Brennan, a former atmospheric physicist with
NASA, has devoted much of her life to studying the aura and
energy systems of the human body. In her book, *Hands of Light*,
she discusses how the mind, emotions, body, and the seven levels
of the aura interact to create balance or imbalance. "Everyone has
an energy field or aura that surrounds and interpenetrates the
physical body" (Brennan 1987, 5). At her New York school,
Brennan teaches her students to both perceive the auric field and to
effect change in that field and in the person as a whole. Changing
the energy in the aura can lead to improvement on many different
levels, from the emotional to the spiritual.

Aura Imaging Photography

Until recently, however, very few people have had the ability
to use this connection between aura and body. Certain clairvoyants, spiritualists, and intuitives seem to see disruptions in the
energy around a person and often give very accurate descriptions
of the problem underneath that energy disruption.

In 1980, an American engineer and inventor, Guy Coggins, developed a camera which could detect and visually display the aura, or energy field around a human being. Known as aura imaging photography, this technique produces a full-spectrum color representation of the aura. The aura camera measures human energy patterns much like a traditional biofeedback device (Coggins 1996). In biofeedback, various sensors are used to measure GSR, skin temperature, and other physiological changes. The results appear on a monitor, and the subject can experiment with altering the readings through meditation and conditioning similar to biofeedback training to change these detected values.

The following chapter provides the reader with an in-depth look at the aura camera and other technology which is aiding people in their search for auras.

Mr. Coggins' research has indicated that his Aura imaging photographic displays using these measurement and evaluation techniques closely resemble the human auras observed by psychics who claim to see human auras. The resulting aura photographic display thus serves as a metaphor for the energy field or aura as observed by psychics who can "see" the auras.

AURA IMAGING PHOTOGRAPHY
Photographing the Aura in the 21th Century

-5-

C. E. Lindgren, DLitt

I discovered my colors last week. Not the color of my skin, my favorite color or my school colors. I saw the colors of my aura, or the energy field that surrounds me.

Mary Tolan, *Arizona Daily Sun*

Today there is a new form of aura photography which many believe is far superior to Kirlian's energy transfer printing. Known as Aura Imaging Photography, this technique produces a color print of the subject. The resulting photographs show the upper half of the subject surrounded by clouds of colors. The upper half of the body is targeted mainly because more auric activity seems to take place in this section of the body. In addition, filming a small section of the body provides better visual observation of color, shape, variations, and distributions. See the photo inset in Chapter 7 for aura photographs taken with this method.

The aura imaging system uses traditional biofeedback measuring techniques. The camera displays the aura as colorful fields of light. The color, shape, and size of the aura can indicate emotional and spiritual changes. Thus, aura imaging photography can provide massage therapists and spiritual energy workers with a tool for quick recognition of conditions and step-by-step monitoring of the subject's progress during the session.

In this technique, a power source charges the subject's body with a very low voltage signal. The signal is then picked up by probes and electronically converted into an aura image and recorded by the camera. Colors and their corresponding spiritual energy states include passionate and joyful red, happy and creative orange, disciplined yellow, sensitive and solitary blue, relaxing violet, and spiritual white. (See Chapter 6 for more information about colors and emotions, and Chapter 10 for information regarding color therapy.) The photograph is a metaphor for the aura.

Guy Coggins, a researcher and designer in this new technology, is inventor of the Aura Camera 6000, which he introduced in 1992. The camera, according to its inventor, does not actually "see" auras. Instead, it produces them electronically—converting energy signals into an auric image with the help of a computer program. These images can then be viewed on a projection screen or photographically printed, creating a permanent record.

Coggins' first aura camera measured the aura by transmitting radio waves through the subject via a hand plate. The computer then "converted the waves into electrical energy which could be processed . . . as light and color" (Coggins 1994). If you were to have a photo taken with this camera, you would place your hands on a probe which transmits a radio frequency through your body. You would then actually begin emitting radio waves at specific frequencies. Your body would become a "living antenna." The energy produced by this "human antenna" is received by a complex series of receiver/scanners located in a grid array behind you. Each probe has a unique receiver wired through a high speed multiplexer. This device converts information from the antenna grid to a computer where it is processed and displayed as electromagnetic energy—in this case, colors.

Coggins later discovered that he could achieve similar results with a less cumbersome design that measures energy level changes directly from the hands. With this design, the antenna and receiver array behind the subject is not necessary as with Kirlian photography.

Recording the Aura

It has long been known that body energy (interstate) changes can produce physiological changes. These transformations include changes in a subject's skin, such as impedance, chemistry, dielectric constant, and the collection of free ions on the skin surface.

In Barbara Brennan's book *Hands of Light* (1987), she explains some technological experiments validating the existence of the aura. A year later, in 1988, Richard Gerber, M.D. states in *Vibrational Medicine* that the search for a scientific tool to prove auric existence must also include Dr. Valerie Hunt's auric research (see Chapter 4) and that of Hiroshi Motoyama. Dr. Motoyama's research indicated the existence of a Chakra-nadir system (i.e., energy transformers). Through his experiments, he was able to measure the bioelectrical fields of psychics and others who had activated a specific chakra during meditation or spiritual enlightenment. According to Dr. Gerber (1988), "the amplitude and frequency of the electric field over the chakra being concentrated upon [by the psychic] was significantly greater than the energy recorded from chakras of control subjects."

Dr. Carlo Montanari, a biologist with a Ph.D. in medical statistics, has also been researching subtle energies in his Milan, Italy lab for over two years. One of the tools he uses is the aura camera. Six thousand photos later, Montanari (1996) says that "the photograph according to our opinion gives an image of the superficial and deep contents of the psyche, and therefore of his/her energetic "egg" and energetic interrelationships with the surrounding environment. . . . We think that the aura photo is reproducing the energetic field around a person (by) sensing the nervous patterns from the hands."

Whether in a still format (print), a video, or a finger or toe print using Kirlian technology, there are basically two methods used in observing these energy centers and auric emissions. The first is the video method where an antennae grid (a sequential series of 100 x 100 radio receiving antennas, each capable of picking up signals closest to it) is placed behind the subject upon which energy is transmitted. The second technique measures changes in skin conductivity levels at various acupuncture points on the hands (using hand probes). These points are correlated to produce an aura image as observed by psychics.

The Future of Aura Imaging

Although the aura colors change with time and situation, the photographic technique captures them at any given moment for analysis. For example, photographs taken before and after massage, chiropractic techniques, and other activities will often reveal dramatic changes in the colors, size, and shape of the aura image. The changes in colors can provide more information than a simple skin meter reading. By visually reading a person's aura, one can determine his general state of tension or relaxation, the balance between left and right sides of the body, and other details about his emotions and spirit.

Many spiritual energy workers, Reiki practitioners, and others are using aura imaging as an educational tool. Aura imaging should NEVER be used to diagnose medical or psychological problems. Ongoing research is being done to match particular patterns in aura photos with specific spiritual states. At this time, no controlled clinical trials have been conducted, and the only studies which have been completed are anecdotal. "Before" and "after" photos of subjects treated by massage practitioners can demonstrate the level of relaxation that has been effected by "hands on" manipulation by the professionals.

Although still experimental, aura imaging technology has been used. As a parapsychological tool, the instrument seemed to verify readings made by certain psychics and mediums. Aura cameras provide psychics, massage professionals, and spiritual mediums with one more tool to evaluate their client's spiritual energy situation. The camera is also capable of recording some behaviors in interpersonal relationships (i.e. sexual attraction, disinterest, and personalities), as with Kirlian techniques, but has not been clinically validated as a tool to be used by psychologists, counselors, or psychiatrists. As a result, the Aura camera should not be used for medical or psychological professionals.

The scientific concept behind this technique is that when two people who like each other touch, their skin resistance drops. On the other hand, when people who have no emotional attraction touch, skin resistance increases and a barrier (an energy line, appearing as a bright section of light) is formed. An example of this was presented in an article on Kirlian photography appearing in the German magazine *Esotera* (Progen 1990). In this study, a man and woman were asked to place their fingers close together for a photo taken by the Kirlian apparatus. This photograph was to be retaken during each of three consecutive weeks. The initial picture showed that the man was attracted to the woman—a strong, bright red and blue corona was photographed around his fingertip. The woman's corona, however, revealed that she was disinterested in him. It formed an energy barrier between her electrical field and his. By the second week, the man's corona changed in shape and size (larger, more intense), showing his persistence. The barrier around the woman's fingertip lessened and began to show signs of red-orange (desire or pleasure). This meant that she was becoming more responsive to his advances. In the third week, the photograph showed two healthy, bright coronas, full of red, blue, and white—blending together. According to the article, the couple is now living together "happy ever after" (Progen, 1990).

By using the aura camera, individuals may be photographed together, with the subjects kissing or touching. An alternative method is photographing the individuals separately while having them think of each other. The photographs are then compared. According to Coggins (1994), the camera can also "show comparative differences and improvements in a patient's energy field in 'before' and 'after' photos taken during spiritual counseling sessions." The session in these cases was performed by psychic or chakra practitioners. In this setting, a photograph was taken before the session and again after the practitioner activated the specific chakra in the subject's body which, according to the practitioner, was the source of the psychic or spiritual problem. After the spiritual counseling, there appeared to be significant increases in amplitude and frequency of the electric field directly over that chakra point (Progen 1990).

The WinAura Video System

Guy Coggins' experimentation has now produced a full-body video image: an aura video. This system also combines traditional biofeedback measuring with computer analysis. The video displays the aura as colorful moving fields of light. With the video technique, the immediate effects of a spiritual balancing session can be seen in the energy field as the session progresses.

Coggins says that one video system is based on the antenna grid design of his first aura video camera. The subject places her hands on transmitting antennas. "The effect is as if you placed your hand on the antenna of your portable telephone," says Coggins. "The radio energy will flow through your body and be emitted in all directions. We scan our receiving antenna in such a way as to form an image. It's like an x-ray of your aura" (Coggins 1996). Coggins believes this technology will be most effective for personal growth and self-discovery. "The visible aura can reflect a patient's spiritual response in real time. The aura reader and subject can see his spiritual energy reflected in the colorful field. It effectively shows not only the energy shifts but also so called 'energy blocks.' The interactive computer talks through its speaker and can tell you if there is a problem. The computers can also listen, so you can talk directly to a machine that appears to be very intuitive" (Coggins 1996).

Interactive Aura Imaging

Coggins will use an interactive computer program which can walk you through questions and give you vocal feedback on the changes happening in your energy field. "The computer might take you through a relaxing exercise—it may ask you to tighten the muscles in your right arm, and you would see the colors change and move on your right side. After the computer asks you to relax, you see the corresponding cooling in color tones. You can see how tension and stress affect your energy field," he says.

An interactive spiritual color feedback program might ask you specific questions about work or your relationships. When you begin thinking about something that creates tension in your life, you might see the colors explode like Fourth of July fireworks. "Many of us fall into old patterns of saying 'Oh, it's just fine,' when we really have unresolved issues," says Coggins. "This technology can help you bring those issues to the surface and deal with them in a gentle way" (Coggins 1996).

THE COLORS IN YOUR AURA

-6-

Jennifer Baltz

The aura is the manifestation of "Ch'i" or Universal energy. Known as our light or rainbow field, it flows from within and radiates outward, through the chakras of the body.

Janice Dye, Reiki Practitioner

By now, you're probably wondering what certain colors in your aura can mean for you. Aura colors can tell a psychic a lot about you. Creative talents, intellect, passions, present loves, future creations, spirit guides, and even your past lives can all be seen in the colors of your aura. The colors are actually vibrations of energy, swirls of light beams moving through the aura. While each color has certain general associations, it can mean different things for different people. For instance, a lot of green energy in an aura might mean that the person is experiencing a period of growth and change. Or, it could mean that this person is a caring social worker or a teacher. The interpretation comes by looking at the mental image pictures that are attached to the color.

Colors are guideposts—they can give you a general idea of what is going on. To flesh out that general picture requires an open mind and a sense of neutrality about what you see. This is why it is easier for psychics to read other people than it is for them to see their own "stuff." It's hard to be neutral to a situation when you're sitting in the middle of it. Sometimes, too, someone may interpret colors for you in a way that does not quite feel like you. This is often because you may remind that person of a friend or situation that is close to his/her heart.

But emotions provide valuable clues when using color as a self-discovery tool. That very lack of neutrality to your own situations can work to your advantage if you ask yourself questions about how you feel, and why you feel that way. As you read more about the colors, notice how each one makes you feel. What is your favorite color? If you find yourself wearing a certain color most of the time, it can mean one of two things. Perhaps you need more of that color in your aura, so you subconsciously surround yourself with it in order to call it in. Or, perhaps you are ready to release that color, and you are wearing it (again, subconsciously) to remind yourself that it is on its way out the door!

Colors you may find yourself releasing can reflect old habits or memories that do not serve you anymore, or the remnants of an old relationship you have finally decided to let go. The general rule of thumb is that if the color makes you feel bright, happy and alive, it is what you need at that time. If the color doesn't do much for your spirits, or if it just seems like what you *should wear*, it is probably a color that is releasing from your aura.

How you feel about certain colors can also give you clues about what you need to learn this lifetime. Do you love pink but dislike yellow? If so, yellow probably contains some answers for you. There may be something about the emotions and energy associated with yellow that you need to deal with. For instance, yellow is often seen as an intellectual color. It relates to mental clarity. If as a child, one of your teachers invalidated your intelligence, the color yellow might bring this issue up for you.

In his essay *Auras*, Edgar Cayce (1945) notes that people are the least neutral about the primary colors in their own auras. In other words, if you have a lot of blue in your aura, you might have expectations, judgments, or strong feelings about the color blue. It makes sense—again, if you're sitting in the middle of anything for a long period of time, it is tough to be objective about it!

The Frequency of Color

Ultimately, everything is made of energy vibrations—your body, the chair you're sitting on, the air you breathe, the water you drink, the sound of your friend's voice on the phone. Quantum physics tells us that we are made mostly of space and waves of energy particles. Quantum field theory takes this concept a step further and says that there are fields of energy which interact with each other and create particles with each interaction (Zukav 1979). "Solid matter" is really a sea of dancing energy!

The entire range of electromagnetic fields, or waves, is called the *frequency spectrum*. Longer wavelengths are at the bottom end of the sale.

Going up the frequency spectrum, the next level is heat, then sound. Human beings can hear sounds that range up to 16,000 hertz. Well beyond that range, from between 500,000 to one million hertz, energy is produced on very short wavelengths. Energy in wave forms can travel through space without needing wires to transmit it. This is the range where radio waves are transmitted, and it is why you can receive a radio station with an antenna or satellite dish simply by matching the frequency with your tuning dial (Fisslinger 1994).

Just above short wave radio on the spectrum is television—the energy waves generated by a television station's transmitter can be picked up by an antenna, a satellite, or your cable company. This is the range of visible light—or light that you can see with your eyes. The colors range in vibration from lowest to highest: red, orange, yellow, green, blue, violet, and ultraviolet. Coincidentally (note Chapter 11—Chakras: Wheels of Color and Light), the traditional colors for chakras *appear in the same order,* from the first chakra (physical energy) to the crown (spiritual energy). Interestingly enough, people associated these specific colors with the chakras *centuries before* modern science discovered wavelengths and color spectrums!

The Aura and Color

The frequency of the aura is just beyond visible light, beyond the range that our physical eyes are used to seeing. Howard and Dorothy Sun (1993), in their acclaimed work, *Color Your Life,* propose that auric energies vibrate around all living things, absorbing sun and atmospheric light. The light is reflected just like a crystal prism reflects sunlight into a myriad of dancing colors. So the aura may actually *reflect* the colors that psychics see, just like a rainbow is really a reflection of light off water molecules.

Colors and Their Meanings

Because we humans are highly visual, the colors we see can have a profound impact on our moods. Observed colors can stimulate our energy, make us wildly happy or just plain content.

Keep in mind that the interpretations listed here are for general reference. Each individual has unique blendings and vibrations of color. And, you will find that your aura can change colors. Often, there is a baseline set of colors that you have *most* of the time. You can change that temporarily, or even permanently if you experience a major shift in your life. You can learn how to change the energy in your aura through meditation and other spiritual practices.

Red: Force of will; passion; vitality; desire; excitability; intensity of experience; physical activity; stress; sometimes anger.

Red is an active, fiery, physical energetic color. People with red in their auras are ready to take on the world. They will not hesitate to fight for their beliefs and their freedom. Force of will and passion are key here. A lot of red in the aura indicates a person who loves to push the limits and live life in the fast lane.

Dark or muddy red may also indicate unresolved anger or stress. If a lot of deep or bright red is seen in the aura over time, it could mean that the person is probably on overdrive and may be out-of-balance. This person might need to slow down a little, or his body may do it for him through setbacks in life.

Orange: Creative; artistic; fullness of experience; urge to achieve and succeed; expressive; playful; sensual.

Orange is a creative and artistic color. It represents creative energy with some mental direction and focus. Orange is stimulating, vital, fun, and playful. People with a lot of orange will be creative communicators—you might find them as artists, writers, or sales people! Orange shows an ability to communicate with feeling and a sense of fun. Orange can indicate a great sense of humor as well!

Yellow: Sunny; exhilaration; flexibility; expectancy; original; intelligence; mental clarity; competition.

Yellow is active and spontaneous. It is the color of mental activity and intelligence at work. Yellow is the color of joy and enthusiasm as well. A good deal of yellow in the aura can indicate a mental profession—a businessperson, lawyer or accountant, for example. Students often show a lot of yellow in their aura when they are studying for final exams! Yellow can also mean looking forward to the future with excitement and joy.

Green: Growth; teaching; endurance; balance; perseverance; self esteem; self love; empathy.

Green has been called a color of growth and rebirth. Since growth is often a matter of bringing energy into balance, green is often seen in an energy worker's aura. Green can also indicate a natural born teacher.

A lot of green in the aura often indicates that a person is processing a big change in his or her life. Many psychics call it a "growth period," or a time when things change and settle out. In a growth period, you take a step in personal evolution. The balance that green brings helps to ease such times of personal turmoil: it means that you may be on the road to something wonderful!

Blue: Communication, unity, depth of feeling; peace; spiritual love; grace.

The cooling, clearing effects of blue are quite soothing to body, mind, and soul. It is an excellent color for meditation and intuitive activities. Blue can help you see things from a more neutral perspective. A predominance of blue in the aura indicates intuition, deep reflection, and spiritual growth. It also shows a person who is looking for the truth and his or her own inner centeredness and/or spiritual path. Many psychics and mystics report seeing images of Mary, mother of Jesus, bathed in blue light (see Church reference).

Indigo: Universal nature; awareness of the truth; clairvoyance; unlimited knowledge; deeply intellectual or spiritual.

Indigo is a deep blue, almost in the purple range. It is the color of inner vision, of clairvoyance, and spiritual work. Indigo stimulates awareness on many levels, from the physical senses to intuition and psychic abilities. Indigo blue can help stimulate a conscious connection with universal consciousness and the Akashic Records (a cosmic "library").

Violet: Mystical; enchantment; charm; deep spiritual understanding; magic.

Violet is a mixture of blue, a color which symbolizes unlimited knowledge, and red, which represents activity and power. People with an abundance of violet in their auras are magical, sometimes mystical, and have a deep capacity to turn inward. Violet in the aura means a person who can create entire worlds in his or her imagination. A writer of fantasy novels might have violet energy in his/her aura. Violet also indicates the ability to create a magical, beautiful home. It suggests strong insight and psychic ability, and the ability to become a charismatic spiritual leader.

White: Spiritually motivated; spiritual channel; expansive; prayer; out-of-body travel; unity.

White has long been considered a color of deep spirituality and enlightenment. It represents all of the colors. At the Aesclepion Trance Medium Abaton in California, pure white is used as a color for trance channeled communication with spirit guides.

People with a great deal of white in their auras are often bored by the mundane details of life and may seem eccentric or whimsical to those with more physical colors. White can show a strong spiritual ability, particularly as a channel for spirit guides, and as a spiritual leader. It can also indicate a chameleon-like personality. Actors often have this color in their auras, and it shows their ability to "channel" a different character for every role they play.

Gold: Forgiveness; joy; abundance; freedom; goodwill.

Gold is the color of forgiveness. It contains much joy and abundance, because in forgiveness there is no scarcity. People with gold in their auras inspire others with their optimism, goodwill, and generous nature. Gold is not a color for holding grudges: it is rather for moving on through life freely and enjoying what is given. Gold indicates a spontaneous, childlike innocence and a desire to share with others. Its creative and fun-loving nature opens up many possibilities. Gold is also an excellent color for protection and self-protection.

Interpreting Colors

Note: do *not* take these meanings as absolute. We humans have many special qualities. The most important one is that we are all individuals. In terms of our aura colors, no two are exactly alike.

We all wear colors differently. Within your aura, the colors can have different meanings as well. Treat these interpretations as a guide only. If you notice that certain colors predominate in your life—you wear them often, or tend to use them in your home—you can ask yourself which meaning fits you. Sometimes, though, you can get too much of a good thing. Too much of a single color can cause an imbalance. Inner guidance, also known as intuition, will let you know.

QUICK COLOR GUIDE

Infrared: Intensity, powerful emotions, leadership, passion

Red: Challenge, action, power, demanding, fast pace
Pink: Tenderness, love, caring, longing, romance
Light Red: Joy, eroticism, sexuality, sensitivity, femininity
Red-Orange: Desire to be center of attention, charisma, entertainment
Orange-Red: Confidence, creative expression, activity, originality

Orange: Creativity, enthusiasm, joy, happiness
Golden Orange: Fun, self-confidence, hard work, enthusiasm
Gold: Forgiveness, goodwill, abundance, prosperity, shining light

Yellow: Happiness, excitement, openness, playfulness, curiosity, intelligence
Yellow-Green: Compassion, idealism, teaching with joy

Green: Counselor/teacher, growth, hard work, ambition, gentle strength, empathy
Turquoise: Compassion, sensitivity, practicality, teacher, soothing, guide
Aquamarine: Spiritual seeker, peacefulness, sensitivity
Light Blue: Tranquility, peace, idealism, spiritual light, religion, inner quiet

Blue: Communication, intuition, rest, loyalty, wisdom, devotion, service

Indigo: Clairvoyance, spiritual truth, abundance, imagination, neutrality

Violet: Cosmic knowledge, faith, meditation, magic, imagination
Lavender: Elfin-like amusement, fun, lighthearted, spontaneity
Blue-White: Communication of spiritual ideals, angels, spirit guides

White: Spirituality, Divine energy, channeling, unity, enlightenment

By Susana Madden

THE INTERPRETATION OF AURIC COLORS USING AURA IMAGING PHOTOGRAPHY

-7-

Guy Coggins and Susana Madden

Auras are like a signature, each as individual as the person they surround.

Gina Allan, author of *Gifts of Spirit*

The purpose of this chapter is to provide the practitioner or researcher the opportunity of understanding the various colors, and their meanings, as interpreted by the Aura Imaging Camera. The same color analysis may also be used by psychics and others in viewing the various aspects of the human aura.

It should be emphasized that the color analysis forms a "blueprint" of how the various colors can and, in most cases, should be viewed. The aura camera should NEVER be used to attempt to diagnose or treat any suspected medical or psychological condition. The individual in question should immediately seek help from a trained and licensed medical physician, chiropractor, or psychologist, who is able to provide the appropriate diagnosis and care. This help comes from many avenues including family and general physicians, physical therapists, surgeons, gynecologists, orthopedists, other traditional medical practitioners or alternative health, and medical care. It is, therefore, not the purpose of this color analysis to replace therapeutic (mental, physical, or emotional) analysis.

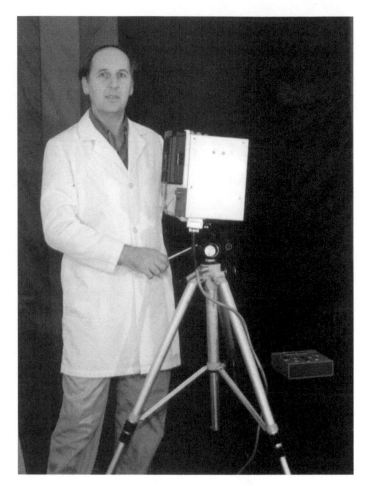

Guy Coggins, inventor of the Aura Camera

Auric colors provide us with an alternative in understanding our emotions, consciousness, energy processes and centers, and the inner spiritual Self. In obtaining a color analysis, one should always seek the assistance of a trained and experienced Aura Imaging technician.

Meanings of the Auric Colors

Every color has its unique qualities and purposes. Imagine a color wheel. Each color is a location on the wheel. No color is better than another. Each has its inherent lessons, its positive and challenging traits. Please note: these definitions do not apply to children.

The right side, picture left of the aura photo: indicates one's expressive active or masculine side, the personality one projects outward and how other people see us. The color in this position is indicative of the persona or how we project ourselves to others. This part of the picture also represents the recent past. If there is no color in this position or a hole, so to speak, this may indicate a loss of some sort, or a wish to let go of the past, perhaps a recent move, or a profound personal transformation. A hole may indicate a great and abrupt change of some sort.

The left side, picture right of the aura photo: indicates one's feminine, receptive, or feeling side, the part of the personality that receives, feels, accepts, and imagines. The color in this position is also indicative of what one is creating for him/herself in the near future. If there is an abundance of color here, the person may be focusing most of their attention in the future. If there is a lack of color here, the person may be dwelling on past memories and events.

The center of the aura photo, above the person's head: indicates what the person is experiencing in the present moment. If there is a band of color stretching like an arc over the top of the photo, this indicates what the person's hopes, goals, and aspirations are. For example: an indigo or blue arc may indicate the person's highest aspirations to be spiritual or artistic. A red arc would indicate more monetary or business goals.

Auras that expand out: indicate spiritual expansion, expressiveness, extroversion, social activity, desire for connection, gregariousness, positive outlook, sense of adventure.

Auras closer in: indicate inward focus, sensitivity, desire for solitude, meditation, peace, tranquility, or rest. This could mean a need to express or to move out.

Ultraviolet: This color may mean one of several things: you may be experiencing a time of stress, or most likely are being inspired by startling and profound visions. You have "genius," meaning you are able now to think thoughts that have never been thought before. Your psychic abilities are phenomenal. You may shock people with your incredible insights and clairvoyant abilities. You are truly a "child of the new age." You may wish to channel what you see into a new and unique art form or some amazing new invention, or who knows? Your highest goal is to manifest into the world what you see in your mind's eye.

Violet: You are the fairy or leprechaun person of the color spectrum. "Magical" would best describe your life and your way of operating in the world at this point. You would rather talk about miracles, magic, and pots of gold at the end of the rainbow rather than anything ordinary or mundane. You would rather focus on the ethereal and the sublime. The beautiful world of the imagination is where you feel safest and happiest. You create a magical environment to live in. Your psychic abilities are also strong and fine-tuned now.

Light violet: At the present time you may be experiencing a profoundly magical spiritual awakening. White, an actual mix of all the colors of the rainbow spectrum, represents intense spiritual transformation while violet symbolizes vision and clairvoyance. This mix of these two shades indicates that you are going through a supercharged, magically synchronistic growth period. The energy of those around you may be instantaneously raised just by your mere presence.

Lavender: You sparkle and glow with a mysterious inner light. Not only are you a magical, elfin/fairy-like creature, seemingly of another world, you are also a natural, clear conduit for spiritual energy. In your present, balanced state you channel pure, divine, white light and inspire others. You have a need for quiet, harmony, and peace in your life, allowing plenty of time for rest, reflection, and meditation. Your primary focus in life at this point is spiritual. Much of the time, everyday matters hold little importance compared with your spiritual and meditative activities.

White: You are a natural, clear conduit for spiritual, unifying, creative energy. In your present balanced state, you channel pure, divine, white light and uplift others naturally. You may be operating from your crown chakra. You walk the magic path. Profound bliss is yours.

Blue/white: "Peace, love, and transformation" best describe your focus in life now. You are a natural, clear conduit for spiritual energy for others as well as yourself. This light-colored blue indicates you are in a regenerative, restful phase. If you do not work in the holistic arts, you may find yourself gently encouraging and nurturing others without thinking about it. Presently, your highest goals are to achieve complete inner peace and to develop your relationship with the Creator.

Light blue: Spiritual, sensitive, peace, and loving best describe your focus in life now. This light-colored blue indicates that you are in a regenerative, restful phase, but, at the same time, you are channeling the divine white light which indicates you are acting as a clear, spiritual conduit for others as well as yourself.

Blue: At this point in time, you are experiencing deep inner peace and tranquility in your life. Above all, you want to create harmony and ease in your environment. You may be on vacation or just experiencing a "time out" to relax and gather your energies. If you meditate, you may be able to easily access blissful states of consciousness. Your spirituality, rest, and peace are your main focus now.

Aquamarine: You have a compassionate, sensitive, and peaceful nature, yet you know how to focus yourself in order to accomplish your goals. You are a natural teacher, counselor, energy worker, and parent. You know how to help, encourage, and nurture others with equal amounts of firmness and affection. People respond to your sensitivity and caring and naturally want to confide in you. You may find yourself presently in a period of transition and change.

Turquoise: You have a compassionate, sensitive yet practical nature. You are a natural teacher, counselor, artist, and parent. Presently, you may find yourself in a "time-out" phase, needing time to be alone, rest, and recuperate. Self-nurturing is essential for people who are constantly giving to others. Time for a bubble bath.

Green: "Hard at work" would best describe you now. You have serious goals, and you live your life in an organized, deliberate, and economical fashion. You are ambitious and desire prestige, noto-riety, and power. You are also full of compassion and can be just as generous as you are demanding. You may be an excellent teacher, counselor, social worker, business owner, or cause fighter. You are full of gentle strength and altruistic ideals.

Yellow/green: Compassion and idealism mixed with a sense of joy would best describe your present focus in life. You have serious goals and ideals and have natural compassion towards all of humanity, yet you wish to enjoy yourself while you work. You have a bright and quick intellect always curious for new ideas. You may be a voracious reader, gobbling up every book you can get your hands on when you encounter a new subject interesting to you.

Green/yellow: Compassion and idealism mixed with a sense of fun would best describe your present attitude toward life. You have serious goals and ideals and have natural compassion towards all of humanity, yet you wish to enjoy yourself while you work. Just because you're serious about accomplishing something doesn't mean you live your life seriously. You're fun to be around, and you inspire others with your happy, hopeful attitude.

Yellow: Joy and happiness surround you now. Your excitement is contagious, life is your playground, and you make everything fun. Even the most tedious of household tasks becomes a game when you do them because you infuse everything with a sense of playfulness. At heart you are a happy, laughing child. You also have a bright and curious intellect hungry for new and exciting ideas.

Gold: Prosperity is yours now just for the asking. Luck, abundance, and joy surround you. You inspire others with your warm, optimistic, and happy attitude. Your goodwill toward everyone you encounter triggers a chain reaction of love, acceptance, and friendship. Your whole being radiates like sunshine, and others look to you to lift their spirits.

Golden orange: Joy and creativity are what you wish to focus on at this point in time. Friendship, socializing, having fun, and being yourself are present goals most important to you now. You make your work and chores a pleasure and strive to enjoy every moment. You have a great sense of humor and laugh easily. Your life is a fun, creative project.

Orange: You can't help expressing yourself creatively! You are an artist at heart and march to the beat of a different drummer. Right now, you are feeling powerful. You have the energy, enthusiasm, confidence, and will to accomplish anything you desire. This is a time to "go for it." If you have any original ideas or creative projects in mind, you need to begin them now! Orange is also the color of originality and independence.

Red/orange: Right now you are driven to express yourself! You want to bring out and promote your creative ideas and inspiration. You now have the confidence and certainty to stand on your own and show the world who you are. "Creative" and "dynamic" would best describe you. You are a lively and entertaining companion and usually find yourself the center of attention in most social situations. You may be an inspired entertainer or artist or perhaps an entrepreneur with an original product. Whatever you do, people are entranced by your charisma and originality.

Orange/red: At this point in time, you are driven to bring out and promote your creative ideas and inspiration. You have the confidence and certainty to stand on your own and show the world who you are. "Charismatic" and "inspired" would best describe you now. You may be a popular entertainer or artist or perhaps an entrepreneur with a unique vision. Whatever you do, people are entranced by your charm and originality.

Red: At this time, you are experiencing a time of challenge with an action-packed schedule, barely leaving you time to breathe, let alone sleep. You have a lot to do, and you have the energy and power to move mountains at this point in your life. You may find yourself acting as a dynamic leader or find yourself in the limelight or the center of attention. You are definitely being noticed. You have so much energy you sometimes don't know what to do with it. You may exhaust the people around you with your incredible enthusiasm.

Infrared: You may be experiencing one of several things: you may be feeling stressed, or most likely you are experiencing a time of intense activity, feeling powerful emotions to the extreme. You may be feeling so ambitious and full of energy that you may even forget to sleep. Your entire being is a volcano of passionate life force energy exploding in many directions. Your social life and career thrill and inspire you at the present time. Your dreams are coming true. With a band of this color arching above your head near the top of the photo, you aspire to have many exciting, adventurous, and passionate experiences.

Note our extensive color section regarding the different auric configurations. These individuals, shown in this section, are from all walks of life. They have one thing in common, in that they exhibit through their aura photograph a variety of brilliant colors, based on their spiritual goals and developments. From violet to red, the camera allows the subject and psychic practitioner to analyze the different moods and developments of these varied individuals.

CRYSTALS AND THE AURA

-8-

Susana Madden

When each of the seven chakras are open and balanced the aura will appear to be clear and radiate like light refracted through a crystal.

Andrine Morse, author & columnist

"A magical crystal can change your life forever, Susana," said my friend as she gave me a quartz crystal pendant on my birthday. Little did I know then that her words would prove to be true, and that her little birthday gift would change my life in the most mysterious ways . . .

Ancient alchemists, seers, and metaphysicians have been aware of the magical amplification and magnification properties of quartz crystals for eons. These beautiful stones have been used for centuries to aid in divination, connect with the divine energy of the universe, and link us with the astral plane—the dimension where we go at night to dream. Linda Goodman, in *Star Signs* says that the ancient Atlanteans could record more than 500 hours of voice data on a crystal the size of a fingernail. And today, we use quartz crystals in our watches and clocks to keep time.

In recent years there has been a resurgence in collecting clear quartz crystals and using them as tools for spiritual growth and adornment. Many energy workers use crystals in their work of aligning and balancing the human energy field—the aura.

Catalysts for Energy Transformation

Crystals actually have something in common with our auras. They can act as energy transmitters and transformers. This is why many gypsies, fortune tellers, and other psychics have used the crystal ball to help them see the past and future. The clear crystal actually helps them to "tune in" like a radio, to psychic pictures, information, and images floating around on the psychic plane. Many spiritualists and readers do not need the crystals in order to do their work well, but using the clear quartz crystal or crystal ball helps them "tune in" to the colors and images and stories contained in a client's aura more easily and quickly.

According to Joy Gardner in *Color and Crystals*, crystals not only transmit energy, they also amplify it. They are charged with whatever energy we put into them, and they transmit this energy outward into the atmosphere or the aura of another person. This is why holistic practitioners like Barbara Brennan (author of *Hands of Light* and *Light Emerging*) sometimes use crystals to draw out foreign energies from their clients' auras.

Just like our auras, these clear stones are able to pick up and store energy from other sources. Crystals can actually store energy for long periods of time. If not cleaned, crystals will store the energy of the places in which they were kept, as well as the aura energy of their owners. Large, clear quartz crystals not only add beauty and a sense of balance, but they also raise the spiritual vibration, and store the energy of your living space, when placed throughout the house as decorations. They will also soak up, like sponges, any unwanted energy lingering in the atmosphere and can therefore help to reestablish harmony in the environment.

Dreams in a Crystal

How can crystals change your life? Each one has different properties. Traditionally, different crystals are used to balance different chakras, different layers of our auras. They can evoke profound changes. Do you remember the crystal I mentioned at the beginning of the chapter? It was a clear quartz pendant with another "baby" crystal inside it. The stone reflected rainbows when held in bright sunlight. To me, it felt like a wonderful talisman of good luck. I wore it consistently, even during sleep.

The first night I wore it I began having vivid dreams of a beautiful place. I had never dreamt of it before, yet it felt as homey as my own back yard. There were mountains, with winding trails. I followed them through lush jungles and forests full of chirping birds and multicolored flowers. People passed by dressed in brightly patterned embroidered clothes. During my dreams, I wandered through whole villages with people sitting at huge looms working patiently day and night. Night after night, my dream self walked and experienced life in this beautiful, artistic place full of my favorite colors. It wasn't long before I realized I was dreaming of Guatemala.

Shortly after I received the crystal, my financial situation greatly improved. I received a large insurance settlement from a car accident that happened several years earlier, plus a surprise interest check from my insurance company. My tax return arrived early with an extra $100 rebate check I had not expected. I was also given a substantial raise at work. To top it off, I found $55 in cash lying on the sidewalk in front of my house when I went out to sweep it!

When I told my friend about my change in luck and those dreams of Guatemala since she gave me the special crystal, she laughed and said, "Susana, didn't you know that clear quartz crystals with a "baby" one inside help a person manifest on the material plane? I could tell you needed a little help in that area. That's why I gave it to you." My friend also told me that she bought the crystal from a Guatemalan man at a flea market, who was wearing the crystal. He parted with it quite reluctantly. She believed that my Guatemalan dreams were caused by his energy which had been absorbed by the crystal. I was just tuning into it on the astral plane. She said, "If you want to stop dreaming of Guatemala, you'll need to either bury the crystal or soak it for a couple of days in order to thoroughly cleanse the energies. Apparently, his vibrations are still very strong in the crystal."

I decided against my friend's advice about cleaning the crystal. I was enjoying my astral connection with Guatemala. Not only did I continue dreaming of the place, but I also started seeing symbols, weavings, and color patterns in my nightly explorations. In my spare time, I began drawing and painting what I saw in my dreams. Before long, I had accumulated a huge body of work, too much to store in my small cottage. To my surprise, a local gallery owner I approached fell in love with my colorful, abstract pieces and arranged a one person show for me. Every painting and drawing sold, with a demand for more! Almost instantaneously, I found myself with a lucrative new career and was able to quit my low paid preschool teaching job. All of these changes began with the delicate crystal I wore around my neck.

Using Crystals to Enhance Your Energy

Since that first crystal, I began collecting clear as well as colored quartz crystals and use them for many purposes. Try using your crystals in the following ways. Place them in the middle of a meditation circle to help focus your energy. Put one under your pillow at night to assist in remembering your dreams. Wear them as jewelry to balance and strengthen your electromagnetic field. Drop a clear quartz crystal in a glass of water, place the glass in direct sunlight for an hour, and enjoy a sparkling, high energy drink. When you're sad, lie down and place a clear crystal on your heart center to lift your spirits. When far away from a loved one, exchange personal crystals. This will help in keeping your telepathic channels open to each other when you are far apart.

Finding Your Own Crystal

How do you find a crystal that is "right" for you? Each one is unique and carries a different vibration. It's important when purchasing a crystal to find one which will blend well with your own personal energy field. A crystal can balance and energize your aura. The crystal you're naturally and immediately most attracted to is probably just the crystal you need to help balance your auric field.

Follow your own intuition when bringing a new crystal into your life. Hold each new stone in your hand and simply feel the energy. Does it feel prickly, strong, soft, energizing, or calming? Which stone feels the best to you? Which one stands out, or attracts you strongly? Many people today wear clear quartz crystals as jewelry for fun as well as to strengthen their personal auric fields and enhance their overall spiritual energy.

Since crystals absorb energy, you may want to clean your crystals regularly by either soaking them in purified water, burying them overnight in the earth or a bucket of sand, or by placing them in direct sunlight for several hours. Purifying a crystal in this way releases any foreign energies the stone may have picked up.

Mysterious, magical quartz crystals are the Creator's gift to us, as a reflection of our highest potential, a tool to help us realize our spiritual magnificence. Crystals can help us learn about the nature of our aura and remind us of that rainbow within.

LOVE COLORS

-9-

Susana Madden

What is energy? Energy is Love and Light and consciousness. How do I increase my own energy? Increase Love . . . turn on the element and direct your Consciousness inwardly.

Janice Dye, Reiki practitioner

Wouldn't it be exciting to know at first glance what kind of mate that attractive stranger might be? First appearances are often deceiving. Unless you are familiar with a person's background, it usually takes quite a while to truly know someone. On the other hand, the aura tells all. The aura does not lie or conceal. The beautiful colors in one's auric field can reveal a person's true nature like an open book. Your aura is completely individual, like a thumb print. It reveals a lot about a potential partner's relationship skills—as well as your own!

The old saying "opposites attract" certainly holds true where auras are concerned. Sweethearts under the age of thirty often choose mates whose aura colors and personality are opposite their own. It's because we often unconsciously wish that the other person will make up for our weak points, rather than develop those qualities in ourselves. Have you ever dated someone who seemed completely opposite from you? A partnership or marriage of opposites can sometimes be difficult. Since your life experience is so different, it's a challenge to communicate clearly.

After the age of thirty, we often tend to choose someone with an aura color and personality similar or the same as our own. These unions can be much happier and enduring, since your views and values are more alike.

A person may have one or several different colors in their aura, but one color will usually predominate. This color describes one's general personal makeup. Remember that the aura is a vibrating field. The colors may change dramatically due to stress or a big change in that person's life. Usually, the colors return to the original pattern when the person returns to a more balanced state.

By taking thousands of photos, and asking many questions, I have found that the six basic colors seen in the aura correspond to six general personality types, with each having a distinctive social and sexual style. If you know what color his or her aura is, you have a better idea of what to expect. Do you want to be with a lusty red? Or would you rather be with a supportive and sensitive blue? Here are the six basic colors along with their general descriptions. Please note that these descriptions do not always apply but are generalities, or likely tendencies. People often have more than one strong color in their aura, and they can exhibit a combination of these traits.

RED: Reds usually love sex. For them it's a hearty, wanton, playful, and joyful physical release. Reds don't necessarily need to be in love to enjoy sex, since sheer physical pleasure is the most important thing. They are passionate lovers and are not afraid to fully experience their sexuality and turn their fantasies into reality! Red signifies high energy, physical and emotional drive. If you want to have an exciting fling with a partner who takes control, choose red.

ORANGE: Oranges need space. If you're consumed in your career or need a lot of time for yourself, choose a partner with a lot of orange in his or her aura. An orange is fun when (s)he's around, and also loves adventurous, high-energy sex like a red, but an orange will not be too demanding. People with orange auras are usually extremely creative, independent, often athletic, and frequently need to take off on some high adventure or jump full-bore into a creative project to test their limits. An orange might ask you to go sky diving or bungie cord jumping.

YELLOW: Yellows love to sit around and discuss, theorize and analyze. You'll often find them hanging out in bohemian cafes, huddled around steaming espressos—enthusiastically debating how to solve the world's problems. To them, life is one great mental riddle that can be solved in a logical and systematic manner. Innately curious, a yellow is always asking questions. Like *Star Trek's* Mr. Spock, a yellow's approach to life is primarily mental and cerebral. A yellow would probably rather discuss your political views on a first date than ravish your body. If you are turned on by intelligence, quick wit, and an optimistic attitude about life, go with Mr. or Ms. Yellow.

GREEN: Greens come from the heart, and their generosity and compassion know no limits. They are often innately caring and want to save the world. Greens can be doctors, nurses, teachers, therapists, and social workers. They want to serve and make the world a better place to live in. Greens make tender, loyal, caring lovers, as much concerned with your pleasure as with theirs. They also tend to love children and animals, enjoy domesticity and family life. Greens can also be ambitious—striving to reach the top of their field. Not only kind, this person is often financially well-off.

BLUE: Blues are sensitive. They have a great depth of feeling and crave intimacy and meaningful communication. They are often thoughtful and introspective. Blues are not usually material-istic: a rich, spiritual, contemplative, and creative life is more important to them than monetary wealth. Above all, blues wish to be in loving, supportive relationships to which they can generously give and reveal themselves. With blues, love and sex go hand in hand. If you want to be with somebody who is true and emotionally there for you, choose a blue.

PURPLE: Expect the unexpected with a purple! These fasci-nating nonconformists live in the wonderful, wild worlds of their unlimited imaginations. Often purples would rather daydream and fantasize about sex rather than actually do it. Fantasy and role playing are not out of the question for a purple. Purples, who tend toward passivity, usually enjoy physical intimacy only after they feel safe and trust a caring partner. If you want to take the lead in a relationship and explore your fantasies, then purple may be for you.

FUCHSIA PINK: This vibrant color sometimes appears in a particular part of the aura or may color the entire field. I don't define this color as a category, but rather as a sign which indicates the person is falling in love, or about to. Fuchsia pink also represents universal or unconditional love. Often, people who are very close and spend a lot of time together will "match energy" and their auras will look almost identical. Their energy fields vibrate to the same frequency, and are in balance. Partners in such relationships will feel very comfortable and in harmony with one another. The energy of love also vibrates at a very high frequency rate. When one is in love the aura expands and intensifies its color and brilliancy. Isn't it always easy to tell when someone is in love? Their whole being seems to sparkle and shine, and they look more alive. You're actually noticing and responding to their extra vibration.

PLAYING WITH COLOR

-10-

Barbara Martin

Throughout the ages there has always been the employment of the Colour Wisdom to establish poise and harmony, to soothe and sustain, to restore, and to create anew.

Roland Hunt, *The Seven Keys to Colour Wisdom*

Have you ever stopped to take in the radiant colors of flowers or the lush green of trees in the Spring? When you look at fluffy white clouds against a clear blue sky, do you feel uplifted and renewed? Our Earth is brimming with colors: colors that affect our emotions and our energy. Color can make us feel excited, reborn, enthusiastic, mellow, angry, passionate, or a whole host of other strong emotions.

Holistic practitioners and artists from the beginnings of humanity have used color to affect moods and influence action. Kings wore royal garments of purple and gold, designed to impress their subjects with their divinity and leadership capabilities. Priests and priestesses often chose white to symbolize purity: nuns and priests today wear black or black and white for austerity and simplicity. Playwrights have set the mood of their productions with color since theater began. Dark sets and furnishings give a sense of mystery and foreboding. Bright, colorful sets tell us the play is a musical or a comedy.

With your understanding of the aura and chakras, you can see that color goes farther than mere psychology. When you surround yourself with particular colors, you tend to match those colors with your aura. If you surround yourself constantly with gray walls and wear gray clothing, your aura may take on shades of gray. Too much gray often leads to fatigue.

The subconscious mind plays an important part because it is "picturing in," or registering these colors and creating them in the aura. We have to understand, too, that we ourselves are color. We radiate color from every aspect of our being as light and energy. So, the colors we see in the outside world make a strong impact on our consciousness. Often, we bring the colors around us right into our auras.

We choose colors by our moods. If you're feeling joyful, you will wear brighter colors. If you're sad, you tend to go towards black and gray, even though what you really need is an uplifting color to help you get out of that funk. Notice how people dress at a funeral? They dress in black for the occasion because black is considered the color of sadness. But black tends to anchor in that sadness because it sits in the aura. Wearing black can actually prolong the grief and suffering. Given its effect, is black really the best color to wear for that situation?

The ancient Egyptians recognized the importance of color, and they always surrounded themselves with bright hues for various purposes. The Chinese and Japanese have also been very color-conscious throughout the ages. The ancient Chinese art of feng shui holds that certain colors can be used in specific locations in your home to create more wealth, happier relationships, and so on (Baltz 1995).

So, it becomes very important to choose colors that are right for you in the present moment. Fashion traditions dictate certain colors in certain situations, but they may not always work from an energy point of view. If browns make you moody, do you really want brown upholstery inside your car, where you spend hours every day? If red makes you restless, it's not a good color to choose for your bedroom. If you tend to feel sulky, you might consider eliminating black clothes from your closet.

Choosing Your Best Colors

How do people choose colors? Each color has a certain frequency of energy, both physical and spiritual. We absorb that color and energy, accordingly. Outgoing people often like the lighter, brighter hues such as reds, pinks, yellows, warm blues and greens. These types of people are very open to their outside environment. People who are more introverted will go more to the cool colors, such as the ice blues and forest greens. Those who prefer the darker, moodier shades often have a detached attitude towards the world, and often are happiest on their own, away from society and other people. However, if you are introverted and would like to be a little more outgoing, you can try wearing extroverted colors from time to time, or use them as accents in your home.

What These Colors Can Do For You

Red

Red represents life. It encourages enjoyable body activities, like eating zesty foods, dancing, passionate relationships, and fun. Notice the red foods such as cherries and tomatoes. If you want more courage, zeal, passion, and fire in your life, try wearing more reds. Red and orange can add energy and vitality as well. If you want to calm down or reduce tension in your life, consider wearing less red. Red in the pastel shades, like pink, is a feminine color. Pink is best for loving reactions. True red is more masculine and shaded deeply, such as ruby red or maroon.

People who wear a lot of red often make quick decisions and judgments on their own. They're impulsive. Many times, they're also tense and nervous or stressed. If you're dealing with someone who tends to wear a lot of red, or has these characteristics, try wearing calmer colors like blue or green around them. This can help to give them focus and balance.

Orange

Orange energizes the body. It isn't exactly a popular color these days in clothing—people don't wear much orange, but they should. Orange puts things into motion. It helps build energy and gives strength and endurance. It connects one very strongly with life. People who wear orange tones, including orange, peach, and salmon, are people who demand action and have the mind to back up that action. They can be shy, but they still go out and get what they want. Orange can boost your creativity and your sales ability as well. The reason is that it ties emotion and language together—it helps you express your feelings. Orange is a good color to use in a creative workroom or near your writing desk, if you aspire to be published.

Yellow

Yellow is more of a mental color. People who wear a lot of bright yellow will be very analytical in their processes. Their minds are razor sharp. They know how to use their body, and they move well. They can be talkative, funny, active, and sometimes very picky with details. A school teacher would benefit by wearing yellow to encourage clear thought in her students. You can also wear a little bright yellow any time you want to think clearly, such as when taking a test. Bright, clear yellows are best for this—muddy or brownish yellows are not mentally stimulating. Yellow is an excellent color to paint a study area.

Green

With emerald green comes a perfect balance between the mind, the nerves, and the body. It is a color of growth and abundance. Wearing green helps you to be outgoing, optimistic, and energetic. People who favor green live practical, down-to-earth lives. They like to live close to nature. Apple green is a good color to build intuitive awareness and clarity. People who wear green are usually very successful financially. Wear this color if you want to borrow money!

Blue

Wearing blue can aid in relaxation and in seeking spiritual truth. Rich royal blue shows honesty, good judgment in material affairs, and often indicates someone involved in science or art.

Blue shows your integrity, sincerity, and natural wisdom. Many psychics also see clear deep blue as the color of clairvoyance. Powder blue can inspire you on a creative level. Turquoise brings good luck and a feeling of abundance. Electric blue is an excellent color for performers.

Indigo and Violet

Indigo is also very good for a person who is teaching. It is an elevating color, and most people see it as a very spiritual color. Wearing indigo can help stimulate your qualities of being realistic and brilliant in your outlook towards life. It can also help you hone your skills in whatever profession you pursue. Indigo is a very good color to maintain inner strength, power, and spiritual strength. There is tremendous depth to indigo, and wearing it or including it in your decor helps you to discover the spiritual depths.

If you've lost someone you love, purple is an excellent mourning color. It gives deep peace to the soul, which is much more comforting than the traditional black. Purple helps soothe the nerves. Lavender and violet work well, too.

White

There is an old truism: "When in doubt, wear white." It works because white is a neutralizer. White is a highly protective color. Pearl white has a gentle, forgiving feel to it, and can help you bring in those qualities. Bright crystal white represents a blending of energy, strength, courage, and vitality. It has all the colors of the rainbow. Use white and soft whites in your wardrobe and your home to feel expansive, clear, and strong in your goals.

Gold and Silver

Gold is also a protective vibration that brings inner strength, wisdom, and abundance. Wearing gold or having it in your home can help you create more abundance and wisdom in all areas of your life. Bright silver connotes intelligence and keen powers of perception—someone who thinks for him/herself. Wearing silver can help you access your higher intelligence and become more perceptive.

Colors for Specific Situations

Social Settings
If you want to be socially accepted in a group of people, try wearing bright magnetic colors that will attract others to you. In this case, it's often best to wear bright shades of your favorite colors, since these are most likely the colors you usually carry in your aura. In other words, they show the true you.

Job Interviews
When interviewing for a job, wear warm tones in your favorite colors. The interviewer will perceive you as a warm person. If you wear cocoa brown, steel grey, or black, that person is not going to be drawn to you. In these colors, you would seem ordinary, and fade back into the group of interview candidates.

Meditation and Psychic Awareness
To open up your psychic abilities, you might try these colors: Clear blue stimulates clairvoyance. Blue tending towards indigo can bring in more spiritual energies, such as past life awareness and connection to the akashic records. Gold helps with knowing on a crown chakra level, and is a good color to visualize when communicating with God. Green, blue and orange can be used in energy work: green energy tends to balance and soothe, blue is good for cooling, and orange is stimulating and vital.

Performing Arts
If you're a singer and you're going to go out on the concert stage, plan your wardrobe accordingly. Deep rose pink and electric blue are two excellent colors to wear on stage. The pink helps to create a loving bond with your audience, and the blue attracts attention and says "I am good at what I do."

At Home
Dusty rose or very serene green carpets help you and your guests find balance and a sense of welcome. In the kitchen and breakfast nook, you might try a bright sunny yellow, or a warm

green to encourage vitality and balance. In your bedroom, use calming and soothing colors such as light violets and pinks, so you can sleep. You don't want an active color that will agitate you just before going to sleep. Even if your favorite color is red, consider calm blues, greens, or pinks for your bedroom to help you wind down at day's end.

At Work

If you have a home office, consider light yellow or pink to feel warm and energized. If you work at a place where you cannot choose wall color, you might bring in some plants with bright, warm-colored flowers, or wall hangings and pictures in those tones to add brightness and energy to your day. If you are going to be in an office situation, you don't want a cold blue wall.

Red is an excellent color to stimulate people to buy. You'll find that restaurants with orange and red have more customers. Chinese restaurants which practice the art of feng shui to enhance their business usually use red as well. It is a color of success. Purple and gold are also excellent colors to bring in more wealth, as is green, the color of growth.

For Relaxation

When you're recovering from surgery, or helping a loved one recuperate, bring in items that reflect the soothing colors you want to use. For instance, you might want to see green or warm blues when you wake up each morning. If you are trying to bring more energy into your body, orange, yellow, bright pink, warm green, and other vital colors can be useful.

Another way we can raise our vibration and the vibration of the environment around us through color is with flowers. They're very helpful. White flowers are especially helpful to clear energy. Red flowers are good if the physical body is down and in need of more energy. Violets and roses are very helpful, as well as geraniums.

Playing With Color

Use the color suggestions here as a playful guide to choosing home accents and clothes. Experiment. As an exercise, walk through your home as though you had never been there before. How does each room make you feel? Does that dark wood paneling feel oppressive, or warm and homey? You'll find it will be different for each member of your household. Check the areas where you spend most of your time. What colors predominate there? How do they make you feel? As you learn to sense and understand the effect of color vibrations in your personal space, in your aura, you can use it to your best advantage. Color, once mastered, can be a very valuable tool.

CHAKRAS:
WHEELS OF COLOR AND LIGHT

-11-

Jennifer Baltz

". . . the basic stuff of the universe, at its core, is looking like a kind of pure energy that is malleable to human intention and expectation . . . as though our expectation itself causes our energy to flow out into the world and affect other energy systems."

James Redfield, *The Celestine Prophecy*

Earth's Power Centers

Sacred places, or power points, on Earth have a special force or energy radiating from them. A power place often feels unsettling or overwhelming because it is a vortex—a connection between one energy plane and another.

Our world has a handful of major power vortices, and millions of minor ones. Sedona, Arizona; Ayers Rock (Uluru) in Australia; the island of Kauai, Hawaii, Stonehenge in England, and Delphi in Greece are some of the major vortices. Spiritual pilgrimages to these powerful energy centers leave you feeling transformed because of the tremendous change they create in your energy field. Some of my most compelling awakenings have come in energy centers such as these.

Human Power Centers: Chakras

The human body has dynamic energy centers, too, just like the Earth. These power centers are called *chakras*. The word chakra means "wheel" in Sanskrit, the ancient religious and literary language of India. And, indeed, people have known about and worked with chakras since the beginnings of humanity. Many cultures, though separated by thousands of miles, associate the same characteristics and colors with each chakra.

Chakras function as energy transformers, just like those power places on Earth. They take in energy from the environment around you and spin it out into your aura and your body to revitalize and energize you. The energy is often changed vibrationally into a form your body can use. Chakras both take in and send out energy. This vital energy flow through the chakras is necessary for day-to-day functioning.

Chakras spin just like wheels. They are about the size of a silver dollar, and they shine with every color of the rainbow. When I look clairvoyantly at a chakra, I see a bright spinning circle of intense color. Chakras are quite beautiful. Sometimes they look like flowers.

Whether you can "see" them or not, you use your chakras every day. When you have "gut feelings," say something from the "bottom of your heart," or know something "off the top of your head," you are feeling one of your chakras at work! Because they act as transformational passageways for energy, they connect our physical bodies with the mental, emotional and spiritual essence of who we are. They link all of these levels together so that we can act as whole, integrated human beings.

Location, Location! Location!

Just as the Earth has an axis (North to South Pole), so do you: your spine. Energy flows up and down your spine, through your chakras, which are centered just in front of the vertebrae (see figure 2 on the next page).

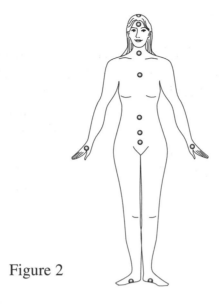

Figure 2

There are seven major chakras up and down the spine, plus chakras in the hands and feet. The chakras spin fast in a clockwise direction. In other words, looking down at your body, your chakras would spin towards your left hand. If you are feeling tired, chances are that your chakras have slowed down and are not spinning quite so fast. Sometimes, chakras slow down because they are a little clogged with stuck energy—it's similar to the air filter in your car getting filled with dust and debris. Other times, a traumatic event in your life will damage a chakra by forcing energy through it too quickly.

Chakras can also open up and close down depending on how much they are needed. If you are trying to visualize how this works, imagine the lens of a camera. You can bring more light into the camera by opening the aperture, or you can close it down if you have too much light. It is the same with chakras (BPI 1989). Say for instance that you are going to the airport to pick up a loved one for a long awaited visit. The fourth chakra will probably open up to give you a deeper connection with that person as he or she steps off the plane.

Chakras and the Body

Many "alternative" schools of medicine such as ayurveda and acupuncture are based on the concept of energy meridians and the chakra system. Different chakras and energy channels in the body are responsible for the functioning of specific organs and areas. When the energy channels or chakras are blocked or out of balance, you in turn become out of balance.

In the physical body, the chakras are said to be connected to specific endocrine glands. These glands secrete hormones that regulate physical and emotional processes in your body, like desire, energy level, and so on.

How Chakras Function

Chakras take in energy, convert it, and then send it out into your aura so you can use it (BPI 1989). Here is an example of chakras in action:

You go into work and notice that everyone there seems glum. All morning long, your chakras take in the "blah energy," and spin it out into your aura and your body. After a few hours, you start feeling "blah", too. Then, you decide to go out to lunch to get out of the glum atmosphere. You go to your favorite restaurant, and your waiter is particularly perky. He smiles and jokes with you, and soon, you are feeling happy and excited again. Your food is good, life is good!

You come back to work feeling upbeat and ready for action. A few hours pass, and you notice that the people around you are looking happier, too. What is happening? You matched the waiter's enthusiasm and started bringing it in through your chakras. Your chakras spin out the positive energy into your aura and your body. Your co-workers are tired of feeling "blah." Once they feel the positive energy in your aura, they match it subconsciously, converting the negative stuff in their own space into enthusiasm. Then, they feel good, too. A little enthusiasm can go a long way.

It sounds too simple to be true, but it works. Why? Let's look at another example. For centuries, philosophers and psychologists have celebrated the power of positive thinking. More recently, Norman Vincent Peale brought the concept back in his book *The Power of Positive Thinking*.

Self-help teachers like Anthony Robbins, Bernie Segal, M. Scott Peck, Dan Millman, Les Brown, and many more have promoted this message: energy and emotions are catching. If you surround yourself with happy people, an uplifting environment and positive thoughts, you can create anything. Anthony Robbins is a living example of this. He went from living in a studio apartment, so small and poorly equipped that he had to wash his dishes in the bathtub, to owning a castle by the sea. He runs a multi-million dollar empire—teaching other people how to do the same thing.

The reason positive imaging works so well is that ability the chakras have to take in energy and spin it out into your aura. The chakras will take in whatever you "feed" them—whether it be positive, happy energy, or sadness. They churn that energy out into your space. So, if you "feed" your chakras positive images and energy, they will spin out that energy into your aura. This is why positive thinking is catching. The more positive pictures you create and spin out into your aura, the more positive your life will be.

To say this in a different way, imagine that you live in your house 24 hours a day, seven days a week. You never leave the property. The furniture, decorations, trinkets, and clutter that you have around you become your world. Say those items are cold or dark, your home is cluttered, and there is no comfortable garden or yard area. Psychologically, you will most likely start feeling depressed or limited.

On the other hand, say you have big sunny windows, beautiful views, comfortable furnishings, a big yard, and so forth. You might be very happy there for a long time and might actually create some pretty wonderful things there as well. Your aura is your home, 24 hours a day, seven days a week—for life. What you bring into it is what you live with until you change things around again.

Simply speaking, the chakras act as doorways to your house. They allow you to connect with the world and bring in energy from it. They also allow you to move from room to room—to connect with all the parts of your space. You use your chakras to link your spiritual nature, body, emotions, and mental processes into a unified whole. When they are spinning properly, your chakras help you manifest your dreams!

Each chakra controls a different part of the body, mind, and awareness. In virtually every culture on Earth, the chakras are associated with the same basic color, emotions, and musical tones. The chakras are also associated with different senses and glands. The gemstones listed are often used to align the individual chakras.

Sometimes a chakra can get stuck, or plugged with "stagnant" energy. This can happen when you are living a repetitive or unfulfilling lifestyle and do not honor your need for growth, change, and variety. For instance, working day after day in a job that does not stretch your creativity or mental processes can cause the energy to become stagnant.

Chakras can also get overstimulated. They get stuck in a "wide open" position, and sometimes they are damaged by too much energy flowing through them too fast. Injuries, stress, trying too hard to achieve, or living too long in a "needy" state can cause overstimulation or damage to a chakra.

The Seven Major Chakras

What follows is information about the characteristics and qualities of the seven major chakras. Special thanks to Dr. Norman Easley, N.D., D.C., L.Ac. for his notes on chakras and the emotions, as well as the Legion of Light *Chakra Awareness Guide,* which is an excellent one-page synopsis of chakras and their functions.

Root Chakra *(also known as base or first chakra)*
Traditional Color: Red
Musical Note: C
Location: The base of the spine
Sense: Smell
Function: Survival, will, self preservation, vitality, passion
Gemstones: Ruby, garnet, bloodstone

The first chakra is located at the base of the spine, right at the tailbone. In many cultures, the *root chakra* (or first chakra) is seen as red. Red is fiery, vital, full of energy and life force. It is a primal body color, and the first chakra is a primal center. The first chakra contains the will to survive, to be. It is the anchor point, or connection with the Earth.

In *Mutant Message Down Under,* Marlo Morgan (1991) talks about rediscovering her first chakra information when she accompanied an aboriginal tribe on a walkabout through the Outback in Australia. In an effort to teach her how to use her first chakra, the tribe made her "leader for a day," and she had to find food and water for the group. For a time, she despaired that they would all die of thirst because she couldn't connect with her natural first chakra ability to find water. When she finally began to open up her first chakra and use this energy and information, she led the tribe right to an underground spring!

Our bodies need to have first chakra stimulation every so often. This is why we go to scary movies, or action thrillers, why we climb mountains and take adrenalin-rushing risks! It keeps the flow of first chakra energy alive and moving. Without it, life becomes dull. When the first chakra is congested, it can lead to feelings of weakness and powerlessness in life—a sense of being ungrounded. Sometimes the first chakra gets overstimulated and the natural fears and concerns related to survival become overwhelming. When unbalanced, one may become obsessed with material security, accumulating things, saving like a tightwad—or someone who is overly concerned with physical safety. The "us" versus "them" attitude can develop with an overstimulated first chakra.

Sacral Chakra *(naval or second chakra)*
Traditional Color: Orange
Musical Note: D
Location: Two inches below the belly button
Sense: Taste
Function: Creativity, emotions, clairsentience (clear feeling)
     procreation, sexuality, sensuality, enthusiasm
Gemstones: Coral, carnelian, gold calcite, amber

The sacral chakra is located about two inches below the belly button. Viewed from the back, it is right at the top of the sacrum. The sacral chakra's traditional color is orange, the color of creative energy. It's no accident that creative energy and the second chakra go together—this chakra is connected to the male or female reproductive glands. Creativity is brought to life through our emotions, which also begin in the sacral chakra. In the most basic sense, emotions lead to life: without desire and love, we would not be motivated to create children!

That fiery feeling in your belly, felt when you desire someone (or when the hero and heroine express their love for each other in the movies) is your sacral chakra opening up. The second chakra creates a strong desire within us for unity with others.

This chakra is also the seat of a psychic ability called clairsentience: the ability to feel the emotions of someone else. You can pick up other people's emotions with your clairsentience. Here is an example of how it works:

I was teaching a class one evening when a young woman came in quite distressed. "I've been crying all day, and I don't know why," Mary sighed. "What is wrong with me?" I could see that her second chakra, the seat of emotions, was wide open and filled with the emotions of other people. The intense grief Mary was feeling was not even her own emotion—she had picked it up from someone else who was desperately unhappy.

Mary is a strong clairsentient. This means she is so open to the emotions of others that she takes them into her body. She feels these emotions as though they are her own. Many people use clairsentience to get a "gut feeling" about something. It's no coincidence that "go with your gut" is a popular expression in business!

When the second chakra is congested or closed down, it can lead to feelings of isolation, a desire to be alone, and sexual inactivity. It can also cause dependency. When it is overstimulated, it causes bouts of intense emotion, an overwhelming need to get attention from others or a tendency to overindulge in food, sexual experiences, and material possessions.

Solar Plexus Chakra *(or third chakra)*
Traditional Color: Yellow
Musical Note: E
Location: Just under the ribcage, at the diaphragm or solar plexus
Sense: Sight
Function: Regulates body's life force energy, mental activity, and self-empowerment
Gemstones: Citrine, gold, topaz, amber, tiger eye

The solar plexus chakra is found in the center of your body, just under where the ribs meet at the diaphragm, often seen as clear yellow. Yellow is a stimulating color, sometimes associated with creative mental activity. There is also an element of spontaneity, excitement, and joy. This chakra regulates life force energy in the body: it determines how productive you are. It is the chakra that can literally give energy and life to your dreams by focusing and distributing your lower chakra energies as they are needed. It is located at your solar plexus, just under where the ribs meet.

The solar plexus chakra gives you a natural drive to compete and excel. It is the chakra of self. When this chakra is clear, open, and spinning well, you feel alert, confident, and energetic. You have an "edge." When it is congested, you can feel emotionally suppressed, confused, and unsure how to take action and achieve your goals. When the third chakra is overstimulated, it can lead to overly competitive and self-centered behavior.

AURA *Awareness*

Since the invention of the first Aura Camera
by Guy Coggins in 1970, Aura Imaging Photography
has been extremely popular at fairs, shows, and expos,
and is now being accepted by therapists, scientists,
and medical doctors.

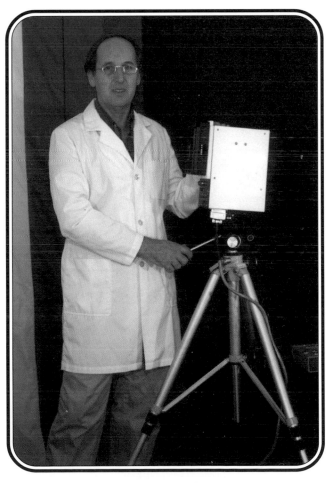

Guy Coggins,
Inventor of the Aura Camera 6000

Energy Imaging

Before ChiGong
session.

ChiGong energy
session.

After ChiGong
session.

Top: Aspirations
Green top experiencing growth

Energy
moving out

Red right:
expressing
vitality.

Energy
coming in

Blue left:
peaceful,
energy
coming in.

Expressing vitality, experiencing growth, expecting rest.

Orange and red: excitement, both left and right, blue band reveals loving thoughts.

Bright ideas: talented accountant, systems analyst, red left shows vitality coming into his aura.

Happy daydreamer: blue reveals peace, contentment, love and affection.

Multifaceted: dynamic orange and yellow top and left—very creative, green right shows teaching potential.

Green to the right: expressing
soothing energy. Orange top,
creative aspirations. Blue left,
sensitive receptive.

Violet white: spiritual personality.
Blue above, peaceful aspirations.

Blue clear communicator top,
sensitive violet coming in,
focused green outlook.

Green: growth, persistence,
endurance, a "stick to it" type.

Peaceful blue being expressed: bringing in and experiencing happy yellow, crimson top, passionate dreams.

Dr. Hidy Hiraoka: ChiGong Master energizing the Aura, see the energy waves.

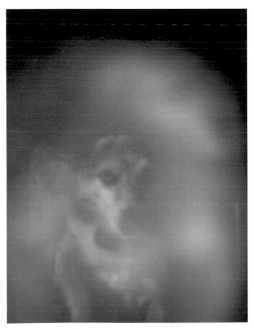

Pet photo: dogs tend to show orange and red, very active colors. Joey shows an unusual rainbow aura.

Golden orb aura: energy moving towards the future.

Infrared: dynamic manager, leader, a natural adventurer, world traveler.

Energized yellow: right and left with violet/ pink, magical aspiration above.

High energy: teenage red aura with intellectual yellow showing above.

Opening up to rainbow vision, experiencing joy.

With Aura Imaging you can recognize soulmates

soulmates' auras, matching energy.

Compatible couple show similar colors

Similar colors often make for an easy-going relationship; however, different colors can reveal a dynamic, complementary relationship.

WinAura Video System by Guy Coggins

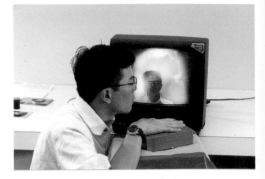

The system shows your aura moving and changing in real time.

Metered display

"Aura Live" by Guy Coggins"

Self-exploration made easy.

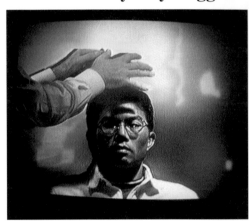

Chakra image

RIGHT SIDE (EXPRESSION) - AQUAMARINE   LEFT SIDE (FUTURE) - LIGHT BLUE

CROWN -
THIRD EYE
THROAT
HEART
SOLAR
SEX - WHITE
ROOT - WHITE

BODY MIND SPIRIT

BODY
MIND
SPIRIT

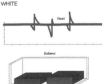

With "Aura Live" you can learn to change others' auras, and everyone can see it happen. If you have bio-control of your energy, you can enhance the clarity and balance of others' energies and watch your progress in their auras.

Graphic display with seven chakra image.

Many businesses are set at a solar plexus chakra vibration. In other words, everyone in the company is supposed to match at a "let's get it done, beat the competition" color (muddy yellow). At first, there is a sense of teamwork—uniting together to create success. But if managers get carried away in that competitive, company-centered (which sometimes becomes self-centered) energy, the demands they place on their employees become overwhelming. Individuals cease to matter in this over-active third chakra environment. The work is everything.

Job burnout can happen when this intense competitive vibration lasts for a long time. Ulcers and other digestive disorders are also symptoms of an overstimulated third chakra. Breaking up the workload with short periods of rest and creative inspiration can help you achieve at high levels without overstimulating your third chakra.

Heart Chakra: *(or fourth chakra)*
Traditional Color: Green
Musical Note: F
Location: Center of the chest, just under the sternum
Sense: Touch
Function: Sense of connection with all things, oneness, caring,
    affinity, love, self-esteem, growth
Gemstones: Emerald, jade, tourmaline, rose quartz

Green is the traditional color associated with the heart chakra—a color of teaching and empathy, and of the Earth. It is the chakra of self esteem and self love, as well as a place of connection with those whom we love. The heart chakra transforms physical desire into love.

The heart chakra is where we store all of those old memories of being unworthy, or making mistakes. Author Barbara Brennan (1995) noted in a workshop that our culture is collectively working on strengthening the heart chakra.

This chakra is also the meeting place for body and spirit. It is the place where you communicate with yourself, and where self esteem lies. A congested fourth chakra can lead to self-conscious-ness, feelings of being out-of-balance, and a narrow focus in life—mainly on the needs of the self. Someone with a congested fourth chakra has a difficult time loving and giving to others. An over-stimulated heart chakra works in the reverse: it can indicate an individual who is more concerned with the group and the welfare of others than his/herself.

Throat Chakra: (*fifth chakra*)
Traditional Color: Sky Blue
Musical Note: G
Location: The hollow of the throat
Sense: Hearing
Function: Communication, talking, singing, higher creative
    arts, divine inspiration, telepathy
Gemstones: Turquoise, blue topaz, lapis, aquamarine

Blue, the color of communication and artistic inspiration, is the traditional color of the throat chakra. This chakra is located in the base of the throat.

The throat chakra governs one's ability to express ideas. Creative energy also moves through the throat chakra, down the arms and blossoms out through energy centers in your hands as written words or physical creations. As a singer, I have noticed that clearing energy out of the throat chakra makes a tremendous difference in the depth, power and range of the singing voice.

The throat chakra also governs the psychic ability of telepathy. Many people in our culture today have trouble voicing their true feelings. Instead of saying what they feel, they just think about it. These unspoken thoughts go out into the telepathic airwaves (also known as the collective unconscious).

Telepathy is the art of communicating thoughts, feelings, and ideas without physically speaking or writing them. Have you ever had a mental conversation with someone in the shower? That conversation is really telepathic communication. The message goes out through your throat chakra, and often actually reaches the other person. The other party may experience what you're sending as a general idea or just a stray thought! Telepathic communication with animals is also possible through the throat chakra.

A congested throat chakra can indicate someone who doesn't like to communicate or has trouble creating with intelligence and practicality. If the throat chakra is overstimulated, it can cause the person to bring in worry and fear from the telepathic airwaves. The person begins to experience those emotions as his/her own, not realizing that he/she is just tuning in to other's mental communications.

Brow Chakra: *(Third eye, sixth chakra)*
Traditional Color: Indigo (dark blue)
Musical Note: G
Location: Just above the eyebrows
Sense: Intuition
Function: Clairvoyance (clear seeing) intuition, spiritual will, connecting ideas, developing a "picture" of the world
Gemstones: Lapis, azurite, sodalite, quartz, sapphire

The brow chakra, or third eye, is perhaps the most well-known of all the chakras. It is located in the center of the head, and is the seat of *clairvoyance,* or clear seeing. Indigo is the traditional color used by the ancients for the brow chakra—it is often considered the color of clairvoyance.

You use your third eye when you close your eyes and see a mental "movie." You also use it to create those mental image pictures I talked about earlier. The brow chakra is the center of ideas and imagination. Without the brow chakra, you would not be able to create your dreams. Why? Because you first need to see, or visualize, something before you can create it. For example, if you cannot imagine yourself starting your own business, chances are that you will never take the steps needed to begin. This is a highly idealistic chakra—it expresses your imagination and desires in their highest forms. There is also a level of abstract intuition here that many engineers and technical people use—the ability to see a solution without going through the logical steps it would take to get there (BPI 1989).

A congested third eye leads to lack of imagination or expression of your ideas. If this center is overstimulated, it creates a high level of idealism, active imagination and constant expression of ideas and thoughts. Too much of a good thing here can lead to dreaming "impossible dreams" like Don Quixote!

Crown Chakra: *(seventh chakra)*
Traditional Colors: Violet, white, gold
Musical Note: B
Location: The top of the head
Sense: Knowing
Function: Knowledge and enlightenment, connection with
    higher planes of consciousness, Divine Will, spiritual truth,
    the divine plan of the universe, certainty
Gemstones: Amethyst, diamond, quartz

You've probably heard the saying, "That idea just came off the top of my head." This is an example of the crown chakra at work. We bring in much of our spiritual information and energy through the crown chakra. Traditionally, the main color in the crown is violet. Violet is the color of mysticism and spirituality. Other colors often associated with the crown chakra are white and gold. White is also a highly spiritual vibration, often used by trance channels—people who allow other spirits to communicate through their bodies for healing and teaching. Gold is the color of forgiveness—many energy workers and psychic ministers see that Jesus used this vibration extensively in his miraculous work (see Church reference).

The crown chakra is the seat of divine will, of certainty, of purpose. Leaders often have especially well-developed crown chakras. They use that certainty on a daily basis in making decisions and giving directions to their followers.

The crown chakra is also your own private doorway into your body. You as a spirit use it as a connecting door between your body and the spirit plane. You leave at night through the crown to go out to the astral plane (dreaming), and return in the morning. Leaving your body at night creates a space for spiritual regeneration as well as physical rest.

When you remember your dreams, you bring that information back with you, down through your crown. Julia Cameron (1992), author of *The Artist's Way,* recommends using a journal, or morning pages, to capture these creative fragments from your dreams and begin using them in your life. The morning pages are essentially a tool to help your crown chakra pull in those astral inspirations.

A congested crown chakra may lead to confusion and uncertainty. An overstimulated crown chakra can create a need either for power and control or a disconnection with physical reality and human relations.

Your Hands and Feet

You also have chakra centers in your hands and feet. The feet chakras are very good at taking in energy from the Earth. The hand chakras can be used to sense energy, to receive energy, or to channel energy outward. Spiritual practitioners use the hand chakras as conduits for the energy which they channel into their subject. For example, Dr. Ostad Hadi Parvarandeh (1996, 9), a famous Iranian energy worker and teacher, says that he is a "medium or conduit through which the energy of the universe flows to other people." This universal energy flows through his hands into the person who is receiving.

ENERGY AWARENESS GAMES

-12-

Jennifer Baltz

For you see, so many out-of-the-way things had happened lately, that Alice had begun to think that very few things indeed were really impossible.

Lewis Carroll, *Alice's Adventures in Wonderland*

Sensing Energy

We live in a wondrous world of interconnected energies. Think of it like the World Wide Web, only on a much larger scale. On the Internet, you can send a letter instantaneously to another person who lives three thousand miles away. You can read articles and papers by some of the brightest minds on the Earth today—who may just happen to live in Botswana, or Sweden. You not only connect with others on the Internet, you interact with them. You may teach them something that affects their lives in profound ways without even realizing it. Or they may give you a life-changing truth. Yet, you have never physically touched, talked to, or even seen each other.

This is how energy works in our universe. Physicists are discovering that particles of energy can affect each other from great distances. These particles even seem conscious—they make decisions about where to move, and then they move there. Are they intelligent? No one knows for sure. Everything is interconnected, interrelated. Everything has an effect on everything else. What you do here, in your daily life, will have a ripple effect that extends out through the world.

This concept applies to thoughts as well as actions. Scientists have done studies with wild monkeys and chimpanzees that prove they are connected on a deeper level than just the physical plane. They work with one group of apes that is isolated from other groups and teach that group of animals a new skill. For instance, perhaps they show them a new way to skin and eat a banana. A short time later, all of the ape populations in the area are eating their bananas in this new way—without having physical contact with each other.

How are they communicating? They may be talking telepathically, showing each other pictures of the new banana eating method. Or perhaps they dream collectively and pass along the new information that way. However they do it, they are in communication; they are sensing each other's energy.

The world is never boring when you look under the surface at the energy relationships between living creatures. There is a living, dynamic world of light and color, of feelings and textures, of dynamic movement and flowing energy. I find that when I forget "to tune in" and simply look at the world in a more material kind of way (i.e. this is a rock, this is a tree, this is a dog), I get bored easily because I am not growing, not learning or experiencing anything new.

Sensing energy is about gaining life experience that will enrich you in ways you can only dream of. To start, remember that baby steps are the way to go here.

Sensory Overload

When you first start these games, you may find that you don't feel or see anything. There's a reason for it, and it doesn't mean that you're not gifted or that you're doing it wrong. It has to do with sensory overload and how you handle it.

We are surrounded by sensory overload. This is a rich world, and we humans have added another artificial layer of games, ideas, and issues on top of nature. We are blasted with these sensory images all day long. Most of them try to get you to do or buy something. When driving in your car, you see sign after sign advertising something. You hear ads on your radio, on television. Walking down the street, you cannot help but notice merchandise in store windows with big sale signs in red and white to get your attention.

You may have noticed that those advertisements are often bigger than life to get your attention. They are brighter, larger, or louder than normal. (Even the cover of this book is pretty bright as book covers go!) Why? Because there is so much input out there that we tune out 95% of it. We ignore it and go on with our lives. Advertisers realize that to get your attention, they have to do the equivalent of waving a red flag under your nose. Since we've learned to disregard almost everything, we have also learned to ignore some of our most basic abilities and sensations.

Energy speaks in whispers—it doesn't shout (except in poltergeist movies). Before you start these energy awareness games, you need to create a quiet, receptive space to perceive those whispers.

Take a few minutes and sit in a quiet place. A restful garden or even your backyard is ideal. Notice the environment around you. Don't think about it—just watch it and breathe deeply. Feel the moisture content of the air, the breeze against your face. Hear the noises. Notice the trees and flowers, the sky, the buildings around you. See all the colors. If you wear glasses, try taking them off for this meditation and notice how much more you become aware of without them. Your field of vision will be wider without the limiting frames.

Animal communication expert Penelope Smith says that if you watch animals, you'll see they are almost constantly in a quietly receptive, alert state. Even when dozing or sleeping, dogs and cats can rouse to full wakefulness and action in a matter of seconds. What you may see as laziness in animals (lying around, sniffing the breeze) is a place of quiet perception, of noticing the details and experiencing their surroundings (Smith 1996). This is the state where subtle energy perceptions are experienced. One of the best ways to find that place within is observing how your animal companions do it.

When you feel calm and present within your surroundings, then try one or more of these games. If you would like to see the difference between your life as it normally is and what quiet contemplation can do for your awareness, try the games before you do this open-eyed meditation session, and then try it after. You will notice a difference.

If you still have trouble feeling energy, give yourself a little time and just notice if you feel anything different. Perhaps your attention might be drawn somewhere else, or within your body. The name of the game here is awareness, not perfection. The more you are aware of what distracts you or overwhelms you, the easier it will be to proceed.

1. Feeling Energy

Preparation

Sit down in a quiet place. Take some time to allow your perceptions of the world around you to expand. Now, rub your thumb gently in a clockwise circle on the palm of your opposite hand. You may feel a slight tingling. Notice if you feel a difference between the two hands. Now, rub your other thumb gently in a clockwise circle on the other palm. You've just begun to open up and activate your hand chakras.

Sending Energy with Both Hands

Hand chakras are small power centers in the center of your palms. They are adept at both sending and receiving (feeling) energy. Decide right now to send energy out of both hand chakras.

Next, move your hands about three feet apart from each other out in front of you. Slowly bring them together and see if you can feel a point where you notice pressure between them. This is the energy coming out of each hand repelling against the energy flow of the opposite hand.

Sending and Receiving Energy

Take some deep breaths and just notice how your body feels for a moment after doing that last game. Are you experiencing any soreness, tightness, or tension in any part of your body? Just be aware of it for now.

Next, decide that you will continue sending energy out of your right hand, and receive it with your left hand. All you have to do is imagine that your left hand is set on receive.

Move your hands at least three feet apart out in front of you and begin bringing them together. Notice what happens as your right hand gets closer to your left hand. What are you noticing in each hand?

Remember, there are no right or wrong answers here. Everyone experiences energy differently. You might feel a tingling, or a pressure; you might notice warmth or coolness; you may feel a texture, or see a flash of light; or you may not notice anything in your hands. All of these are fine responses.

2. Sensing Energy with a Partner

Sometimes it is easier to feel energy when you are working with someone else. Why? Because you are used to your own energy—it is, after all, yours. Another person's energy can be very different in vibration than your own.

Preparation

Decide which person will feel energy first. Both of you can prepare by taking some quiet time as mentioned above, and then gently making clockwise circles on your palms to open the hand chakras.

Both Partners Sending Energy

Both of you simply decide to send energy out of your hands. Then, sit with your hands up, directly opposite each other and slowly move them closer towards each other. Notice when you begin to feel a different sensation between you. Stop to tell your partner when you do. Take a few minutes to discuss what you are sensing.

One Partner Sending Energy

Decide which partner will send energy and which will do the receiving. The Receiver needs to decide to switch over into Receive mode, and the Sender should just decide to stay in Send mode. Compare notes on what the Receiver and Sender notice.

Repeat the game again, switching sides, and notice if your perceptions of the same position (Sender or Receiver) are different than your partner's. Most likely, they will be different. If you are more kinesthetic (feeling-oriented), you will probably feel the energy rather than see it. You might feel it as a warming or tingling in your hands, or as pressure, or as a "presence" of something there. There are no right or wrong ways to feel energy! If you are more visual, you might notice flashes of light or just a sense that "something is there," without really seeing colors.

Try this game with different partners and see what you feel with each of them. Again, your perceptions will probably be different with each person because each of us has a unique energy vibration. Each of us "feels different" on an energy level.

3. The Button Game (BPI 1995)

Materials You Will Need: A small to medium-sized button, sturdy thread

Creating a Pendulum

First, string the button on a piece of thread about 8 inches long. Attach it securely. Congratulations! You've just created a pendulum.

Opening Your Hand Chakras

Now, rub your thumb gently around in a circle on the center of the opposite palm. Decide to open your hand chakra up and ask it to go into Send mode.

Spinning the Pendulum

Next, dangle the button pendulum over the palm that you activated, perhaps an inch or two away from your skin. You may notice that the pendulum starts spinning in a circle. You might need to raise or lower the button a little to get it to spin, depending on how much energy is coming out of your hand chakra. You can also decide to send out more energy to get the button going.

Notice what direction your button pendulum is spinning. That is the direction your hand chakra is spinning. Now, decide to stop the button. Then ask your hand chakra to spin the other way, and watch to see if the button does the same.

If you have trouble getting the button to move, you might try going back to that open, receptive meditation in the beginning part of the chapter. Sometimes it's easy to try too hard at these games, and trying too hard just doesn't work. These exercises take very little physical effort because you are not doing anything physical.

Trying to analyze how it works also makes this type of perception difficult because you are putting your attention and energy into analyzing rather than experiencing. It will be easier if you decide to experience it first and then figure it out afterwards.

AURIC EXPERIENCES
AND EXPERIMENTS

-13-

Ruby K. Corder

For most of my life I have been in a dance with the living seas of energy in which we exist. Through this dance I have discovered that this energy supports us, nourishes us, gives us life. We sense each other with it; we are of it; it is of us.

Barbara Brennan, *Hands of Light*

Seeing the Silvery Fire

When I was fourteen years of age, I sat down in a chair at our country home and stared out into an open field, trying to see energy. At first my eyes just went out of focus. I got frustrated after a while and also sleepy. Soon I was just looking out, not trying. Suddenly, I saw the trees erupt in a silvery fire. I sat there astonished, thinking it was some kind of after-image. Turning from the window, I saw my mother approaching. To my amazement she looked like she was standing in a cloud of colors.

This story by Aljadin,* a noted spiritual practitioner of Chinese healing arts such as Qi Gong, Chi Kung, and Fa Lun Gong, relates his first encounter with aura perception. Many people first see auras "by accident" when they are children. Aljadin says that it took him some time to see them by choice.

Sometime thereafter, I became acquainted with a psychic friend of my mother's who told me to place my index finger to my third eye

and imagine white light flowing into my third eye while saying
"open" mentally. This technique doesn't work unless one is totally
in a relaxed state. I tried over and over to my frustration. It didn't
work. Later when I got into ch'i kung, I learned to direct or push my
ch'i. I carefully direct it into my third eye, charging it open. It was
at this point that I started seeing spirits voluntarily.

Aljadin describes his technique to see auras. First, he says, it is
important to achieve a relaxed state of awareness. Meditation,
sitting in a garden, or subtle energy movement exercises like ch'i
kung can help achieve this state of relaxation. Then, he recommends the following:

> Imagine white light entering the third eye. Carefully direct the ch'i
> (energy) into the third eye. Practicing in a dimly lit room is a good
> place to start. I personally prefer living things, such as plants or
> people as focal points. Then just look. But don't stare. If you stare
> you will get after-images from the exhaustion of the photo-pigments
> in the eye. A good way to test the image you are seeing is to take a
> piece of white paper and place it in front of you after you think you
> are seeing an aura. If you see an image that is similar in nature to your
> focal point, then you are trying too hard and you are seeing an after-
> image. It takes time in some cases.

Even so, Aljadin notes that "still to this day, seeing auras is
more involuntary than anything." In other words, effort just
doesn't work when it comes to spiritual practice. The old Ran-
dolphian** concept of "try and try again" can just give you a
headache when it comes to seeing auras.

A First-Time Experience

Jupiter,* a young girl who just started seeing auras last Septem-
ber relates her experiences:

> I have seen many colors such as: light and dark blue, violet purple,
> neon purple-blue, yellow, green, turquoise, white and black. I have
> also seen mixtures of yellows and greens, purples and blues. I don't
> really do anything to increase my ability to see auras. It just comes
> to me. I can only see auras to their maximum when I'm totally

relaxed and not tired. When I look at a person, usually I just see auric colors, but sometimes I have to concentrate in order to see the colors.

Once again, you can see that effortlessness is a key factor in seeing auras. This is why so many children have the ability when young, then "grow out of it" as they get older and more stressed.

Jupiter says that she started seeing auras as part of a game.

> It all started when my mother and I went over to a friend's house to talk one day. She asked us if we could see auras. I said "not really but I did see a big purple cloud on top of your head." And she said "Wow! Maybe we should look at your mother and you tell me what you see, then I'll tell you what I see." I then concentrated on my mother's head and saw black then white, green and then purple! So I told our friend what I saw and she said that she saw the same thing. From then on I have been seeing lots of colours and watching my parents' auras. Now all of my classmates ask me to tell them what colors their auras are. I do but, the only problem is that I get exhausted rather fast and am forced to stop for the day.

Jupiter "got permission" to see auras because her mother's friend validated the girl's ability and confirmed what she saw. Is it that simple? Is that all it takes to see an aura?

Energy and the Five Senses

Janice Dye, an authority on Reiki spiritual energy techniques, says that many people experience auras with other senses than sight. She believes that all of the five senses can be extended to perceive energy: "Although, not all people are aware of their ability to see auras, we all sense auras, through a combination of senses at a subconscious instinctual level. We are all part of the infinite, and therefore exist well beyond the boundaries of our three dimensional physical form. You do not have to touch a person to feel the heat of the energy emitted through her field. It has been my experience that the block or inability to see this energy comes strictly from our own fears."

Dye says that the aura is a manifestation of universal energy, also known as ch'i or Ki. The layers closest to the body are denser energy—the layers that are farther out are formed of more subtle, or spiritual, energies. "In order to perceive the subtle layers consciously," says Dye, "you must increase your own vibration to the vibration of this level by bringing more light into yourself."

The first step, she says, is to realize that "the physical body is merely energy vibrating at a low frequency . . . we are not solid. Allowing yourself to accept this truth is a release from the boundaries of our limited reality of three dimensional experience."

Dye talks about the human ego as a limit that we must overcome.

> Acceptance of our expansiveness beyond the known reality of the self, is release of the ego. Ego can only perceive from a three dimensional viewpoint, with a concept of "I exist, as I believe I exist." Auric vision is a threat to the ego's concept of self (existing only in your physical form). It cannot be achieved unless fear of the unknown is abandoned through the release of your concept of self.
>
> Intuitively, we begin to feel that there is "more to us than meets the eye." There is energy that is dense, and physical, and energy that is higher in vibration and not visible. As energy is stimulated with more energy, the energy increases its vibration.

Dye compares the relationship between the aura and the body to the relationship between water and steam. Both are made of the same energy, but they are formed differently: "I put a pot of water on the stove. Heat from the stove element concentrates energy directly to the pot of water. The heat energy from the element begins to stimulate and increase the vibration of the water energy. The water energy begins to dance, vibrate and bubble before my eyes. This water energy seems to change as it rises up and transforms into steam. It continues to evaporate until it is no longer visible." Dye says that although the water evaporates, its essence, its energy is not gone. The water itself is no longer visible to the eye, but its essence is contained in the steam that has diffused throughout the air. Dye says that the transformation from water to steam would happen naturally over time even without the heat of the stove. Eventually, the water would evaporate and change form into water molecules in the air. Universal energy is much like the water, she says. "Universal energy is constantly working to effect change, and the transformation of the water is inevitable. It evaporates into the ethers and then showers down again to the earth in droplets of rain in a cyclical experience of eternal abundance of water." Conversely, Dye notes that applying more concentrated energy in the form of heat to the pot of water would cause the pot as well as the water to transform: the heat would melt it.

Dye recommends that we apply this metaphor to our own human bodies. "Your body is the pot. The universe is constantly pouring fluid energy into this container, and as the container overflows it is radiated back out to the universe through your chakras."

Evolving into the Energy

Charles C. Goodin believes that as we humans evolve through time, we will expand our senses to include seeing energy. "Auric vision is part of the overall package of enhanced senses which arise from human evolution/involution. In other words, a heightened sense of consciousness gives rise to heightened senses, one of which is auric vision. As such, it is difficult, and perhaps misleading, to separate auric vision from other enhanced senses. Thus, some people will feel auras, smell them, taste them, hear them, etc." Goodin notes that "Working on a single sense can lead to imbalance. Things which lead to auric vision will probably also lead to other enhanced senses. Followed to maturity, all forms of traditional meditation will lead to an awakening. The problem is that most people only meditate casually and then wonder why they get poor results. A few days or weeks of training is nothing. Traditional disciplines require a lifetime or perhaps many lifetimes to get full benefit."

Like Edgar Cayce in his essay *Auras*, Goodin notes that we color our perceptions of others by looking through our own energy: "One thing to keep in mind is that when I see your aura, I am looking through my own auric field. Thus, my own aura colors my perception of yours. Most people miss this completely. Consider this example: If my aura is yellow and yours is blue, I will perceive yours as green. This is overly simplistic but illustrates the point."

Goodin recommends opening your mind and thoughts to accept a wide range of possibilities. Seeing without judgment or preconception is very important. "Many people who actually see auras convince themselves that they do not because of their own narrow worldviews. Open-mindedness is essential. Then you must still the mind more and more until it is like a deep pool of clear water. This reduces the interference of your own aura and enhances your perception of the aura of others."

Goodin also notes that everything on earth has an aura. "Some people mistakenly believe that auras are a human thing. All things have an aura, including rocks and the air itself." He says that "These are best seen when out-of-body (your spirit essence traveling outside of your physical body), because there is practically no interference by your own physical body and its energies."

Practitioner Carol Beltz also agrees that auric perception is a matter of all the senses, not just sight. This awareness is drawn from her own personal experiences. Over the years, she has come to believe that auric field vibrations are discernible through all five senses. "It was easier to feel the vibration bouncing off of my skin than to actually see an aura," she says. "I rarely see them. I know of people that smell auras rather than see them! I think that we sense an energy field and our subconscious mind interprets the vibration and uses one or more of our physical senses. The subconscious mind may be a gateway to the universal mind. Then, it can sense that which is otherwise physically imperceptible. But we interpret this by way of our senses—our vision, hearing, smell, touch, and taste—because we're most accustomed to those senses."

Techniques to Increase Your Perception of Energy

One of the easiest ways of gaining auric vision is by looking at your own face in a mirror and concentrating on the middle of your forehead. Allow your eyes to relax and go into "soft focus," causing the image to become more and more blurry-as if looking into nothingness. After some trial and error, you may see a vapor or light cloud around your head and shoulders. At first, the vapor will be very faint. The image will become stronger and stronger with daily practice sessions. For best results, dim the room lighting as best you can, and sit in front of a white background.

Another more sublime manner of beholding auras, closely connecting man with nature and his surroundings, is described by channeller Regiena Heringa, author of *The Discourses of Sextus* (volume one). According to Ms. Heringa, "Extend your open hands up against the blue sky with fingers of one hand almost touching the fingers of the other. Gently pull your hands away from each other while looking at the space being made between the two hands. You will see the energy." For another variation of this technique, see the chapter on Energy Awareness Games. Heringa also suggests to "look up into the sky and around a tree. De-focus your eyes an inch or so from the tree. You will see its energy. Don't stare too long, as you will get retina fatigue, which at times is mistaken for the aura."

One of the most mystical approaches to auric vision involves two young American girls. In this childhood experiment, Catherine Bruce (a.k.a. Lapis Lazuli), trained with her little sister Anne Marie by rubbing their foreheads together in gentle circular motions (activating the brow or third eye region). They would then stroke their nose against each other's nose and put their eyes as close as possible together. Sometimes, while doing this "psychical bonding," they would place their palms together and would hear their hums and watch their colors. They would say, "Do you want to play the game ?" "Yeah sure!" "Put your hands on my face and draw your eyes into mine." "Put your nose on my nose." "Rub your forehead with mine. I'll go counter clockwise you go clockwise." "Look into my eyes and I look into yours. Let our eyes become one." "Stare into the eye until we become one. Hold hands and watch. Ooh it's so beautiful. Look at the colors. I can hear our hums again."

The sisters gave up their game when they put aside their dolls. Years later, Catherine was delighted that her fiancé was familiar with the game and quite accomplished at this practice. She believed that she had made it up herself. But her fiancé had learned it from a Yogi in Canada. It provided an immediate intimacy between them.

Interestingly, he had been taught to do it silently from the lotus position, knees to knees, placing the pads of the fingertips ever so close together but not touching them. He began the game by meditative trancing with closed eyes.

Sometimes players see nothing but the one eye, but it is a beginning. Some players feel they are drowning in the being of the other player, and so they pull away. But with continued practice, this game opens the brow center allowing a peek into each other's souls with a view of each other's auras. The revving of the chakras that ensues may become audible enough to add a humming musical background. After staring at the "source" and establishing contact, the energy body can be perceived as light, heat, color, and sound. It is a delightful game for the young at heart; calming, loving, and peaceful.

Conclusion

Some individuals are born with auric sight "full bloomed." For others however, the journey requires open-mindedness, desire, the ability to try while remaining relaxed, and practice. It should also be remembered, as Goodin states, that anger, hate, impatience, restlessness, jealousy, greed, and many other "human frailties" are detrimental to auric sight.

Take your time, and start with about fifteen minutes' practice each day. If fifteen minutes causes fatigue or nervousness, start with only ten minutes, gradually increasing practice. The object is to have fun in your psychic search.

---

* Some of the individuals in discussing their experiences requested that their actual names not be used.

** Dr. P. B. Randolph was the first Supreme Grand Master of the Rosicrucian Fraternity in America. Nearly all of his 60 works and reprints concern the power of "Try." In all matters, however, Randolph emphasized the importance of trying, yet in such a way as not to create tension, frustration, and depression.

HOW TO SENSE THE AURA

-14-

Jennifer Baltz

The very next level of perception is to see an energy field hovering about everything.

James Redfield, *The Celestine Prophecy*

Psychic Children

We're all born with the ability to sense auras, just like the five ordinary senses. Everyone has it, but most people don't use it. Why not?

In *The Celestine Prophecy*, James Redfield's narrator dismisses his first glimpse of a plant's aura: "For a moment, I thought I saw a flicker of light, but I concluded it was just an after image, or my eyes playing tricks on me" (Redfield 1993, 49). He decides not to trust what he has just seen.

Most children have the ability to see auras and energy until their parents or society convince them that they are "just imagining it." Gina Allan (1996), author of *Gifts of Spirit,* says that "in a 1987 survey at a private school in Singapore, 85% of the students, ages ranging from six years to twenty-two, could see the physical aura."

Young people can see energy easier than adults because they have not yet been convinced that what they are seeing is "make-believe," or that something is wrong with their eyes! American society is especially adept at invalidating this kind of psychic perception. Other cultures are often more accepting of extrasensory gifts than we are.

Children who are born with especially strong psychic awareness, or who fail to turn it down when they are very young, can have a difficult road growing up. One young woman I know was hypersensitive to energy as a child. She could see energy flashing around her, and she could hear stray thoughts telepathically. She often finished other people's sentences for them without thinking. Although she hardly studied, she was a straight "A" student in school. She had the uncanny ability to know exactly what was required on tests and in papers in order to get an "A." Her guesses on multiple choice tests were especially accurate. But her talent also brought with it a lot of pain.

Because my friend could see and feel energy that others could not, she reacted to things that other people ignored. Feeling isolated, she began to pull inward, getting a pair of glasses to help reduce her vision,* and separating herself from other children. Even her parents thought she was too sensitive. My friend grew up feeling like an outcast, because our society does not reward psychic children or validate their abilities.

Recognizing Psychic Gifts

Psychic gifts express themselves in different ways. Some people are better at feeling energy (clairsentience). Some are better at seeing it (clairvoyance). Some hear thoughts or spirit guides (telepathy and clairaudience). Some tend to have an inner knowing (claircognizance), and some are very good at changing the energy of a situation. If your son has an imaginary friend, he may be clairaudient. If your child gets tired easily, he or she is probably an energy worker—sending his or her energy out to help fix others. The signs are different for each ability.

Gifts like these are difficult for parents. What would you do if your child began telling stories about people that came true? As a child, psychic Lewis Bostwick accurately predicted the death of a neighbor and told one of his mother's single friends that she was pregnant—making himself quite unpopular among the adults in his life (BPI 1995)!

On a less dramatic level, what would you do if your child talked about seeing colors around people? You might get his eyes checked or tell him to stop making up stories. The child would walk away with the message that what he sees is not really there. Sooner or later, he would turn down his abilities to match your beliefs.

We all have different psychic gifts. Because they are not socially acceptable, we have turned them off, or we use them in ways that are. Gut hunches in business are acceptable. A mother's intuition about her child is acceptable. Feeling the emotions of an unhappy friend is just fine. But seeing her aura—well, our culture is just getting used to that one!

Perceiving the Aura

What does this have to do with seeing auras now? As mentioned in Chapter 1, everyone has the ability to perceive an aura—either by seeing it or feeling it. But we are subconsciously programmed with the notion that it just isn't a good idea to do so.

To begin to perceive the aura, you first need to get past all of the old "stuff" in your head that says a) it's not real, b) you must be crazy, or c) *you need to see an optometrist!* In regard to the last, Edgar Cayce (1945) believed that the increase in people wearing glasses in recent generations is due to *evolution.* That's right. He thought that more of us wear glasses now because our eyes are straining too hard to see auras and energy!

So, how do you do it? The easiest way I know is to *not try too hard.* The harder you try to see an aura, the less you will see. Guaranteed. Seeing the aura is one thing that does *not* benefit from hard work. Your garden may look better after an afternoon of weeding, but trying too hard to see an aura will just get you a headache, and you won't want to try it again. So, with the games that follow, don't do them for long periods of time. Give your eyes and your body a rest. Remember, you are relearning something that is not generally accepted in our culture. Give yourself permission to feel nothing at first, and you may experience more than you bargained for!

Going Back to Childhood

Learning about your aura is child's play. Literally. You are turning on abilities that you had as a baby— abilities that were shut down to varying degrees as you entered the "real world."

I was trained at the Berkeley Psychic Institute, which we also called Psychic Kindergarten. Lewis Bostwick, the Institute's founder, wouldn't have it any other way. He realized that two kinds of people came to his door. First, the beginner, who had a lot of enthusiasm, a few strange experiences, but no experience at this kind of thing. Then there were the professional psychics and mediums who needed to know how to control their abilities— before their abilities got the best of them! Both kinds of people needed to learn basic, fundamental skills—the psychic equivalent of learning to tie your shoes before you start walking, or to look both ways before you cross the street.

Coming "as a little child" to this work has two added benefits:

1) A child can play and have fun. As adults, many of us have forgotten how to do this. How many times this week have you just played for the sake of playing, with no agenda or timetable to control you? If you're like most of us, the answer is *Not very often.* Play is a very high vibration. It is in play that we learn, create, and come up with some of our most profound answers.

2) A child does not need to be right. As adults, we've learned that we have to be right. We have forgotten how to make mistakes. A child makes lots of mistakes and learns from them. When you cannot make mistakes, you cannot learn—no mistakes, no growth. It's that simple. In my growth along this psychic path, I've stopped in places where I forgot that it was OK to make a mistake and come back to the game again. When you assume that your mistakes mean the end of everything, you lose your flexibility and much of your awareness. So, be a child again with me, and let's play in a world of miracles and magic!

Imagination

It's no accident that your third eye, or sixth chakra, is the seat of both clairvoyance (clear seeing) and imagination. We use the same mechanism to imagine something as we do to see it clairvoyantly. There is a very fine line between imagination and clairvoyance! More than once in a reading, I am certain that the wild images I see are my own imagination playing tricks on me. Still, I share them with my client anyway because I never know what they might mean to that person. My client usually gasps and says, "Oh, how did you know that?! You're absolutely right!" So, if you think you're just imagining things, *think again.*

Aura Awareness Games

1. Drawing Energy Pictures (BPI 1989)

Materials You Will Need: A box of crayons, paper, and your imagination.

Ok, it's time to go back to the sandbox. Or, in this case, your playroom. Get out those crayons and paper. I want you to draw people you know, places you've been, your home, your dog, your cat. Stick figures will do just fine—you are not trying to be Leonardo DaVinci here.

After you draw your kitty, ask yourself, "If Fluffy had a particular color of energy around her, what would it be?" Then reach for the first colors you think of and draw those colors around her. Do the same with the other pictures. Draw a picture of your room and ask yourself, what color of energy might be in my room just now? Then reach for that crayon and draw it in.

The key here is twofold: First, do not judge what you see. Whether you like the color or not, just draw it in. Don't try to change it or pick a prettier one. Second, trust what you're getting. If all you see is black, color it black. Always trust what you see. Whether it makes sense to you now or not, *what you see is there.*

What this game can do for you:
1. Loosen up your imagination and clairvoyance
2. Help you to think in terms of colors and energy
3. Change your perspective
4. Learn to see and feel rather than analyze
5. Help you to begin seeing energy

2) Feeling A Plant's Aura

Materials you need: Plants—you can do this inside or outside in a quiet area, so either house plants or garden inhabitants will do nicely.

Gently rub your thumbs in a circle on each palm, opening up the hand chakras, as you did in Chapter 12. Then, approach a plant that is healthy and vibrant looking. With a clear mind (no specific intentions), just move your hands closer to the plant and notice if you feel life-force energy around it. You might have to get pretty close in to feel the energy. Ask yourself, If this plant happened to have an aura, how far out would it be? If there were a color around the plant, what would it be? Notice what you sense, hear, or feel in response to the questions. Whatever answer you get is the right one.

You can try this experiment with sick plants, too. One of my favorite things is to feel the plant's energy, then talk with it or sing to it for a while. Tell it how green it is, how strong it is, how well it is growing, and so forth! I know it sounds silly, but try it anyway! There have been studies that bear out the fact that plants actually have *emotions*. Then, feel the plant's energy again. You might notice that it is stronger or bigger! If you are a "brown thumb," you might perceive that the aura gets a little smaller—plants tend to know when a former plant-killer is in their midst!

3) Sensing Another Person's Aura (BPI 1989)

Materials you will need: An open-minded partner and your amusement. Both are essential.

Stand opposite your partner, at least six feet away. Gently rub each palm in a circular motion with the thumb of your opposite hand to get the energy moving, just as you have done in previous exercises. Then, extend out your hands, and slowly walk towards your friend. What you're feeling for is the edge of his or her aura. Take it slow, and just notice if the feeling in your palms changes. You might notice hot, cold, prickles, an edge, fluffy energy, or just a change in feeling. This is the edge of his or her aura. Notice how it feels to you.

Hint: if you're having trouble, have your friend just decide that her aura is exactly three feet out. Sometimes people have auras that extend all the way to China! If you're already standing in her aura, you won't be able to feel the edge of it! Step outside that three-foot circle and start again.

Be patient, and above all, *don't try too hard*. Remember, have fun with this and say out loud what you are feeling and noticing. It helps to validate the experience.

What this game can do for you:
1. Help to open your ability to feel energy
2. Help to get past the inner "stuff" that says, "this is stupid!"
3. Increase your awareness

4) Seeing Energy

Materials you will need: A white or black background (a wall is fine) and a houseplant

Put the plant against the plain background and step back. Unfocus your eyes (if you wear glasses or contacts, take them off). Glance casually in the general direction of the plant. Look a little to the side, not directly at the plant, and don't stare. Breathe deeply, and just notice if you see a little fuzziness around the plant's leaves, or perhaps a flash here or there. You might see a color, or just a little energy wavering around the edges. Try it a few times, but give yourself a break in between. In other words, don't spend three hours straight trying to see an aura! Take it in stages. I also recommend doing the other exercises first and playing with the tools in Chapter 16 while you are doing this.

What this game can do for you:
1. Open up your clairvoyance
2. Help you become aware of the energy around living things
3. Learn how to trust what you see

5) Making Up Stories About People

Materials you will need: Yourself, your imagination, and a place full of people. An open-minded friend also helps in playing this game.

Begin by asking yourself questions about a person you see. Is he married? Does she have children? I wonder what kind of work she does? Does he have a pet? What is his favorite color? Is she outgoing?

Trust your first mental "answer" for each question. You and your friend can compare notes on your stories, or you can make them up together.

You can also do this with objects. My favorite place to read objects is a museum. I ask myself questions about each piece I'm interested in and just allow the answers to come to me. Touching the object helps, but don't touch if the docents object! When on a past-life pilgrimage to Greece, I discovered that at every monument there are little men who hide behind pillars just waiting for you to touch something so they can jump out and say "Please no touch statue." It can ruin your concentration!

What this game can do for you:
1. Help free up your imagination, and that other ability in your brow chakra: clairvoyance
2. Increase your observation skills

*For an informative look at how glasses actually reduce vision, read *Take Off Your Glasses and See* by optometrist Jacob Lieberman.

AURIC PERCEPTIONS

-15-

Janice Dye

*The unique human field does not merely react or interact; it transacts
because it dynamically makes choices. Here, matter and energy, mind and
spirit, are not really different things, only aspects of an expanded reality.*

Valerie Hunt, *Infinite Mind*

Energy Swirling in the Dark

There are several techniques you can use to increase your
awareness of the energy that flows throughout our world and your
own aura. Try these by yourself or with a close friend and see what
you notice.

Place yourself in a dark room, preferably without any light
whatsoever. Take a few deep breaths and relax, releasing the
tension from your body. As you stare into the darkness, what do
you see? Is it complete blackness, nothingness, or is there something there? As you gently relax into the rhythm of your breath,
look deeply into the darkness. You will begin to notice particles of
light energy, dancing and swirling in the dark. As you continue to
look softly, you might soon be able to notice the patterns of energy
as they take form and shape-shift into different images.

After spending a leisurely amount of time enjoying the cosmic
dance of energy in the dark, light a candle and sit in front of it. You
may either sit cross-legged, in a lotus position, or in a straight back

chair with your feet touching the ground. Keep your spine straight. Concentrate your focus on the flame. With every exhale, extend your attention and energy outward to the center of the flickering light. You will notice how easy it is to see the aura of the flame, the glow from the candle's light as it expands as a halo of light.

As you continue to move your consciousness into the flame, you will notice that this halo expands. Keeping your eyes focused on the flame, you take in the peripheral visions and continue to move your consciousness within the flame. Focusing on this object of light will slow down the thought process and you will sense the stillness within. Without shifting your focus, notice the space between yourself and the flame. See the energy going from you to the flame, and see the energy come back to you. The aura is expanding and the room is now engulfed with light.

At this point, you might want to close your eyes and look into the internal darkness. With your internal sight, see the candle once again burning and glowing, yet this time envision it within your heart. Move your consciousness into the center of the flame within your heart and feel the love energy that is a constant radiance from within. Allow yourself this luxury and be in the energy of Love. (Note: This exercise with the candle can be intensified and increased when practiced with another person. As you both concentrate your focus on the candle you will notice that the flame grows higher and the aura brightens very rapidly.)

Mirror Vision

Now you can practice the same type of focus to see your own aura. Position yourself in front of a mirror (a white background behind you works best) and set your gaze just off to the side of your ear. If this "soft focus" seems like a struggle, you are not doing it correctly. This type of focus does not seem unlike the same blank stare that your vision takes when you are slipping into daydream. In this case, you are in daydream vision with your consciousness fully on your reflection in the mirror. The first thing you might notice is a thin white or yellow layer of light close to the head. As you continue to radiate energy with each exhale, watch as the energy expands. The energy is moving and changing form and is often seen as swirling, as smoke will do as it rises. With practice you will begin to identify colors. Often people will report unusual experiences through this mirror meditation. Facial features might begin to change, or look unfamiliar to you. This should not be alarming or frightening. As you increase your energy and light, your body will be less dense. You may even become aware of subtle changes in your physical form.

When attempting to see another's aura, I suggest that you find a partner with whom you are very comfortable. If the two of you are looking into each other's energy field, you will be able to fully relax and take your time as you let the energy flow and expand. You will not be able to identify the auric field if you are self-conscious or afraid of invading someone else's privacy or space.

Auric Energy Fields in Nature

If everything is made up of energy, then everything must have an aura. The most natural and easiest way to identify the energy field is to go out into nature. Animals, rocks, trees, and vegetation are wonderfully open and receptive to your attention. Sit yourself down in a comfortable spot and take in the light of the forest. Admire the beauty of nature's gifts with the same focus meditation you achieved with the candle. Remember that for most of your life, you have been reprogrammed to see only the very dense energy. You have been taught to look at the solid objects rather than the spaces between objects. Let your gaze fall on the space between objects and notice what is really going on. There is always so much going on in the gaps between matter. There is so much going on between one thought and the next.

Let yourself slip into that space and explore. Your ability to see energy is a completely natural sense. Allowing yourself to simply BE and trusting in your ability to see with true sight, is merely a reflection of being your true self. Let love and light guide your way. Follow your heart as it leads you to the truth.

CLEARING YOUR AURIC FIELD

-16-

Jennifer Baltz

". . . be grateful to the Great Spirit for the life that you have . . . if you sit down and say thank you, you can feel everything opening up all the way up your torso. The light comes in and you radiate light."

Lynn Andrews, Shaman, writer, and teacher

Giving and Receiving Energy

How often during your week do you hit energy "lows," where nothing seems to work right, when you feel tired or on edge?

Karyn, a former secretary, used to feel drained at the end of her day. It took her several hours each evening to "recover" enough to enjoy anything. All day, she gave and gave to her many bosses and co-workers. All of them needed something, and she was there for them every step of the way. But that left Karyn with little time or energy for herself. Not only was Karyn giving her time and attention, she was also giving away her life energy to these people.

Sound familiar? Whether you are a secretary, an engineer, or a plumber, there are times when you will feel as though you have been drained of energy by another person or project. Often it has nothing to do with the level of physical activity you have exerted in the process.

To Give . . .

This is how it works. Your aura has a certain amount of energy when it is charged up and vital. If a person, a project (or even your pet), needs energy, you might tend to give away some of your personal stash. Giving away energy is not exclusive to a "people person," by the way. What it really has to do with is emotional triggers in your space. If that person triggers a pattern of guilt, responsibility, memories of an old friendship or relationship, or even reminds you of your mother, you may find yourself giving your energy to her without realizing it.

I've found myself giving away energy in the oddest places, and to people I don't even know. Store clerks and shopping malls seem to be high on my list. Until I learned how to ground (see exercise later in this chapter), I often got quite tired and disoriented in shopping malls.

You don't have to like someone to give them some of your energy. And you don't have to be in the same room. There is a natural energy interchange between people no matter where you are. It can even happen between family members over a distance— on the telephone or even without one! Often this energy exchange is unconscious, meaning that you are not aware of it. It works based on the concepts discovered with quantum physics. Particles of energy can affect each other even though they are miles apart. And so can people.

. . . And to Receive

You can also receive the energy of another person. Ever felt a flood of warmth flowing into your space when talking with a caring friend, or interacting with your mate? That is the other person's energy flowing into your space. They are giving you a piece of their energy. Spiritual energy workers also channel energy into their patients—only they prefer to use universal energy rather than their own personal life-force energy. Universal energy works much better in a session, and using it means that the sender keeps his/her own energy where it belongs: in the aura!

Sometimes, though, it is easy to take on another kind of energy: the problems of someone else. Have you ever helped your best friend through a personal crisis, only to discover that after the conversation, you felt awful? Not drained exactly, just in emotional turmoil and despair.

This is because your friend had a problem, and you allowed him or her to give you a piece of it. In other words, you took on some of the energy that made your friend feel bad. It happens to us every day, and no one is immune from it.

Exchanging energy is part of the way our world works. We are connected on the energy network of life. Energy and information travel from person to person at high speed. It is normal to take on energy or troubles from someone else, but it is also perfectly OK to let that stuff go again, too. Most of the time we do just that. Some problems tend to stick, though. These are the situations that we just cannot stop thinking about, no matter how hard we try!

There are several tools you can use to clear the aura and revitalize yourself quickly. Here are some ancient techniques to help you have a better day.

Grounding (BPI 1989)

Grounding, or connecting to the Earth, is a technique literally as old as the hills. It is taught by many mystical schools and programs, such as Reiki, Barbara Brennan's course, the Berkeley Psychic Institute, and Rosicrucianism.

You've heard people say, "I felt really grounded," or "His training is grounded in this tradition." Electricians use a grounding wire to divert energy and make it safe for them to work. Grounding is basically what it sounds like: you connect yourself to the earth and allow energy to release down that connection.

There are many variations to the concept of grounding. Tribal peoples and animals are naturally grounded. Our mechanized, high-speed culture has made this a lost art, however, in the "civilized" world. When grounded, one is planted firmly in the earth. Energy flows from the planet through your feet into your body, and helps you to release stress, other people's problems and so forth down the grounding. Being connected with the earth gives you a stronger awareness of your surroundings. How do you think your pet knows when there is going to be an earthquake? Through his connection with the planet, of course.

Any method of grounding is preferable to not being grounded. Why? Because grounding is a tool of safety. It will help you handle difficult situations with greater ease. When you are grounded, you are less of a "push-over." You can own your opinions and your personal space with strength and certainty. You feel more clear-headed and ready for action.

You can be either sitting or standing when you ground. You can even ground lying down, moving in a car, or in an airplane, although it is easier to feel it when you are standing on the earth. Here are the basics:

First, take a deep breath, and notice where the base of your spine is. Remember the chakras? Your root chakra is located at the base of your spine. It is the best place to ground from—it isn't called a "root" chakra for nothing!

The other point is the center of the planet. Some people like to imagine it as a bright crystal, others as fiery lava. Either will do.

Now, just imagine that you are dropping a heavy anchor on a long thick rope, straight from your root chakra, down to the center of the Earth, 3900 miles straight down. Mentally watch it fall, and see it hit the center.

Notice how it feels to be connected to Mother Earth. Walk around a little, talk to people, and see if things feel different or more solid when you are attached to the planet.

You can use other images, too, if the anchor doesn't work for you. A redwood tree, with roots wrapping around the center of the Earth, a giant sewer pipe, a waterfall splashing down to the bottom, or a beam of laser light that cuts straight through to the core of the Earth. Any image that helps you feel connected with the Earth is fine.

Releasing With Your Grounding

Your grounding automatically releases any energy that is not your core essence. In other words, if it isn't yours, it just falls down the grounding. You can release the energy of other people: your boss, your mother, your partner, your pesky neighbor. You can release the energy of projects or obligations: work, bills, etc. You can imagine any situation or person that feels uncomfortable heading straight down your grounding. For realism, try attaching a bowling ball to them—the energy seems to leave my space faster when I do that!

When you release energy from your personal space, don't expect to totally get rid of the person or the problem. But you will find that you deal with the situation differently. A big bill that seemed impossible to pay now becomes something you can handle. Your mother, who was in your face just yesterday, suddenly seems a little more manageable. Your boss gives you a little more room. That project you spent your entire week on leaves your thoughts for awhile so you can relax and play with the children. And maybe you don't feel quite so guilty denying your children the latest gizmo they are begging for. A grounding gives you breathing room.

A few more notes about grounding: Your grounding can never be too big. You can ground anytime, anywhere—even on a plane. You can even ground other people around you, just by visualizing a connection between them and the planet. Or, you can ground your house or car. Grounding is a safe activity—it will never hurt you or anyone else, and it does not involve any "black magic." It is simply reinstating a connection with the planet you call home. Try it, and notice what happens!

Filling Up Your Aura

Just like the oil in your car, the aura can become a "quart low" on energy, too. When your aura has low energy, you can feel depleted and tired. You can also develop thinning spots that become areas where negative energies can come in. It's a good idea to bring in energy each day to replace what you have lost.

The idea of this exercise is to imagine your aura filling up with your own energy. The energy you are calling back into your energy field is the same stuff you have been giving away to everyone else during the day. You're just reclaiming it for future use.

How You Do It

There are a lot of images you can use: a big pitcher, a waterfall, a golden sun, a big ball of blue light—it really depends on what you prefer. For now, let's use the pitcher technique.

Imagine a big pitcher over your head. See it filling with your life force energy. Decide that any energy you have given away is drawn back to you like metal is drawn to a magnet. You may even notice where it is coming from. Sometimes I will see mental pictures of places and people as I gather my energy in from projects, friends, family, old memories, and future expectations. See that pitcher as a magnet for any of your life energy that has gone astray!

When the pitcher is full of your energy, decide what color you would like the energy to be. Take a look in Chapter 6 if you're not sure. How would you like to feel? Sunny and full of abundance? Try gold. Peaceful, spiritual, and serene? Try violet. Balanced and centered? Blue or green might be a good color. Or just pick a color that makes you feel good. Imagine stirring the energy in that pitcher a little—just to make sure all of the energy is now vibrating at your color.

Then, slowly pour the energy into your space. You can close your eyes and watch it come into every cell in your body, energizing and revitalizing you. When your body is full, imagine the energy filling up your aura, too. (BPI 1989)

When to Fill Up

You can stop to fill up in the middle of a busy work day, when you are sick with a cold, before you start your car, or any time when it seems like a good idea. You can never overdo this one. Most of us are always a quart low, so to speak. We are so used to giving to others that we forget to give to ourselves. After all, giving energy to yourself is considered selfish! But selfish is not a dirty word. Be selfish more often—you'll feel happier and less stressed!

What this exercise can do for you:

1. Give you more energy
2. Help you bring in a specific vibration or mood you want to achieve. For example: if you are on hyperdrive and you want to feel more serene, you would bring in blue or violet. You can reset your aura and your moods in this way.

A Lifelong Journey

Energy awareness is not something you get instantly and then never need to learn again. It is a process, an unfolding of revelations and bits of information. Just when you think you really see everything, some new corner of the universe presents itself to you. My answers often appear, when I least expect them, from some unlikely sources. One of my most profound revelations came in a supermarket check-out line! Ask your questions of the universe, and allow your answers to return in whatever form they take.

The exercises presented in this book can be done a hundred times, with a hundred different results. The goal of expanding your awareness is not to be an expert. It is to learn how to be in the present moment, to experience the wonder and mystery of life in all forms.

May joy light your life.

RESOURCES FOR
PERSONAL GROWTH

-17-

Blythe Arakawa

"Would you tell me, please, which way I ought to walk from here?" asked Alice.
"That depends a good deal on where you want to get to," said the Cat.

Lewis Carroll, *Alice's Adventures in Wonderland*

There's no substitute for direct, hands-on experience when it comes to psychic development. If you'd like to learn more about auras, chakras, and your own intuitive or psychic abilities, check out these resources suggested by this book's contributors.

This chapter includes sections on intuitive schools; spiritual healing centers; spiritual travel; books, tapes and related products; as well as our recommended reading list. You'll also find information on how to have your aura photo taken, and how to contact contributors to this book for clairvoyant (psychic) readings, or for psychic investigation and research.

Intuitive Training Schools and Foundations

(A. R. E.) Association for Research & Enlightenment
International Headquarters
PO. Box 595, Virginia Beach, VA 23451-0595
Tel: (804) 428-3588, Fax: (804) 422-4631

A.R.E. is the international headquarters for the work of Edgar Cayce (1877-1945). Study groups and other activities, bimonthly magazine, newsletter, extracts from the Cayce readings, conferences, products, and more. Call for more information.

A. R. E.
4018 N. 40th St.
Phoenix, AZ 85018
Tel: (520) 955-0551
Same as the above A. R. E., works with the Edgar Cayce research & remedies.

Avalon Institute for Psychic Development
Chico, CA
Tel: (916) 891-0805
Teaches basic spiritual abilities and psychic tools, clairvoyance, and features a teachers training program. Also offers seminars around the country. Call for more information.

Barbara Brennan School
P.O. Box 2005, East Hampton, NY 11937
Tel: (516) 329-0951, Fax (516) 324-9745
Founded and directed by *Hands of Light* and *Light Emerging* author Barbara Brennan, the Barbara Brennan School is a respected educational institution. Founded in 1982, the School offers a four-year Professional certification program where students from around the world learn to work with the aura on spiritual levels.

Berkeley Psychic Institute
Berkeley, CA (Locations throughout the Bay Area)
Tel: (510) 848-8020
Beginning energy work and meditation classes, one or two year clairvoyant training program, teacher training. See references to these techniques in Chapters 14 and 16. Call for more information.

Energy Master Seminars
The Robert T. Jaffe, M.D.,
School of Energy Mastery
Tel: (800) 238-3060
Training in the art of advanced energy work, enlightenment, and world service.

HRC
P. O. Box 175
Sedona, AZ 86339
Tel: (800) 338-0112
HRC offers educational experiences for individuals and groups who choose to align themselves more fully with their unconditional love, infinite power, and universal wisdom. HRC offers a three-year school of self-mastery, energy work, and world service as well as several heart-based spiritual energy workshops and gatherings. Call for more information.

Monroe Institute (Interstate Industries)
62 Roberts Mountain Road
Faber, VA 22938
Tel: (804) 361-1252
A non-profit organizational scientific research center. One of the leaders in scientific research. Call for more information.

Pacific School of Intuitive and Holistic Studies
2822 Union Street, Oakland, CA 95408
Tel: (510) 893-5809
Offers a six month clairvoyant training program in the Bay Area as well as seminars nationwide. Call for more information.

Phoenix Psychic Institute
Phoenix AZ
Tel: (520) 395-0651
Meditation, basic psychic awareness skills, and clairvoyant training program. Call for more information.

Power to Move Center for Spiritual Learning
Englewood, CO
Tel: (303) 789-4204

Offers basic meditation, and self awareness classes, seminars, and individual sessions plus a clairvoyant training program. Call for more information.

Psychic Horizons Center
Boulder, CO
Tel: (303) 604-0990

Basic meditation classes, clairvoyant training, and advanced spiritual energy classes. Call for more information.

School for Intuitive Awareness
Taos, NM
Tel: (505) 751-3469

Meditation, basic intuitive awareness skills, and clairvoyant training program. Call for more information.

Scottsdale Holistic Group
7350 East Stetson #128
Scottsdale AZ 85251
Tel: (520) 990-1528

Works with the Edgar Cayce research.

The Southern California Psychic Institute
Anaheim, CA
Tel: (714) 772-8269

Offers meditation, and clairvoyant training classes. Call for more information.

There are many other fine psychic schools and training programs throughout the world. Check your local New Age publications and directories to find them.

Spiritual Growth Centers

Church of Aesclepion
1314 Lincoln Avenue
San Rafael, CA 94901
Tel: (415) 453-6196

Offers spiritual (energy) classes through the laying-on of hands as well as trance-channeled techniques, working with the aura, chakras, and astral body. Services and lectures monthly. Long distance trance-channeled sessions are available on request.

Spiritual Travel

Deja Vu Tours
Berkeley, CA
Tel: (800) 600-3404

Transformational pilgrimages to sacred sites around the world, including England, Nepal, Peru, Brazil, the Philippines, Africa, Hawaii (dolphin adventures, Women in Business retreats), and North America. Experienced intuitive tour leaders. Workshops and events on tour. Custom tours created for your group. Ask about free travel via Travel Partners Program. Call for more information.

Lancelot's Desire Metaphysical Travel
Waimanalo, HI
Tel: (808) 259-8530

Spiritual tours led by Gwen Totterdale, Ph.D. Destinations include Australia, England, Bali, the Caribbean, and Hawaii. Swim with the dolphins, visit crop circles and sacred sites like Stonehenge, Ayers Rock, and more. Channeled sessions and workshops on tour. Call for more information.

Books, Tapes, and Related Products

Barbara Brennan Audio Cassettes (see Barbara Brennan School above for ordering information)

Brennan offers three series of inspirational audio cassettes: *Guided Visualizations*—exercises and meditations for self-awareness; *Channeled Classes*—holographic spiritual energy work and teachings from Barbara's guide Heyoan; and *Lectures by Barbara Brennan*—her teachings on energy science and the path of transformation.

Energy Anatomy
Caroline Myss Ph.D.
Sounds True AudioTapes
Tel: (800) 333-9185

Audiocassette series on the chakras and anatomy of human energy.

Dr. Valerie Hunt
Tel: (310) 457-4694

Dr. Hunt offers auric field sound tapes, lecture tapes, meditations, and more. For more information, contact her office.

Legion of Light
Neil S. Cohen
Tel: (800) 543-9301 or (520) 282-0155.

Offers chakra and color charts. Call for information or to purchase chakra charts or any of the awareness guides.

New Editions International. Ltd.
P. O. Box 2578 Sedona, AZ. 86339
Tel: (520) 282-9574 Fax (520) 282-9730

International publicity and marketing resource service. Yearly trade directory (New Marketing Directory), newsletters, lists, and cooperative mailing advertising. Call for more information.

Recommended Reading and Video List

These books are tremendous resources about the aura, chakras, colors, and spiritualism. You can find most of them at your local bookstore. Many can be special ordered. Out-of-print books may be found at used book dealers or at Aura Imaging Systems.

Aura Related Books

The Aura (first published as *The Human Atmosphere* in 1911) by Dr. Walter Kilner, 1973, Samuel Weiser, NY. One of the first books published on auras. Science-oriented—includes Kilner's observations and data about the aura. Out-of-print.

Aura Reading for Beginners by Richard Webster, 1998, provides proven methods to learn to see, read, and feel the aura.

Color and Crystals by Joy Gardner, 1988, The Crossing Press. Introduction to color theory, the chakras, tarot, and other aspects of metaphysics. Fascinating case studies.

Color Energy ® For Body And Soul by Inger Naess, 1994, Energy Corporation. Booklet on the effects of color, written to accompany their products (oils & bath crystals).

Color Your Life by Howard & Dorothy Sun, Ballantine Books. A good basic book about color.

Hands of Light (1988) and *Light Emerging* (1993) by Barbara Ann Brennan, Bantam Books, NY. Brennan, a former atmospheric physicist, combines science and spirituality in these two works, which are actually textbooks for her school.

How to See and Read the Aura (1993) by Ted Andrews, Llewellyn, New Times Press. In-cludes simple but fun exercises to expand your aura consciousness.

Infinite Mind: The Science of Human Vibrations by Valerie Hunt, 1989, Malibu Publishing, Malibu, CA. An excellent work covering both the science of the human aura and spiritual study.

Life Colors by Pamala Oslie, 1991, New World Library, San Rafael, CA. Oslie works with the same system used by Barbara Bowers in *What Color is Your Aura?* Personality and aura color profile questionnaire included.

Living Rainbows: Develop Your Aura Sight by Gabriel Hudson, Rain Light Technology Publishing. Auras and the effects of color.

The Origins and Properties of the Human Aura by Oscar Bagnall, 1970, University Books, NY. Bagnall continued Kilner's work studying the human aura. May be out of print.

The Power of Color by Dr. Morton Walker, Avery Publishing. How color affects you in daily life.

The Probability of the Impossible by Dr. Thelma Moss, 1974, J.P. Tarcher, Los Angeles, CA. Moss's ground-breaking work on auras, Kirlian photography, and many other psychic experiments conducted in her lab at UCLA. May be out of print.

Seven Mansions of Color by Alex Jones, DeVoross Publications. Another explanation of the colors in your aura.

What Color is Your Aura? by Barbara Bowers, Ph.D., 1989, Pocket Books, NY. Bowers discusses her system of using the aura to understand and type personalities. Explains how the aura is a powerful key into understanding the personality. Interesting, concise, and well organized.

Wheels of Light by Rosalyn L. Bruyere, 1989, Fireside Publishing, NY. Explores the seven major chakras and their importance to our bodies, sexuality and life energy. Interesting information on different cultures and ancient traditions.

There are many other informative books about auras, colors, chakras, and Kirlian photography. Check your local book stores and library.

Aura Videotapes Available from Aura Imaging
The International Aura Symposium Video. Taped in San Francisco, this double video is a rare opportunity to see many of the

world's foremost energy specialists in action, featuring: Anodea Judith, author of *Wheels of Life: A User's Guide to the Chakra System;* Dr. Buryl Payne, author of *Biomeditation and the Body Magnetic;* Carol Rittenburger, Ph.D., known as the leading authority on energy body types; Dr. James Wanless, Scout Bartlett, Guy Coggins and more! Video #004-$24.00 (2 tapes, length 4 hours.)

The Aura Workshop Video. This video is a must for those interested in the interpretation of Aura Photography. See the effects of various spiritual techniques manifest in "real time" as they are produced by the INTERACTIVE sensor, the latest innovation from Aura Imaging. Video #001-$12.00 (1 tape, length 2 hours.)

Aura Imaging Photography Video. This video features the history of electrophotography, how it developed from Kirlian photography to the present real time Interactive Aura Imaging developed by Guy Coggins. See previously unreleased experimental footage, and national TV interviews with Guy Coggins on *Extra,* the *Hawaiian Moving Company, Canadian News,* etc. This video is a must for anyone interested in purchasing Aura Imaging equipment. You get a good idea of what the Aura Camera 6000 is capable of. Video #003-$12.00 (1 tape, length 2 hours.)

TO ORDER: Call Aura Imaging, 1(800) 321-2872. Please add $3.20 for shipping/handling. 319 Spruce St., Redwood City, CA 94063. Fax (650) 261-0193 http://auraphoto.com e-mail: info@auraphoto.com

Aura Photography

Would you like to see your own aura on film or video? Contact Aura Imaging Systems Progen Co. to have your aura photo taken, or find out about aura imaging photography or aura imaging video systems. We offer aura photos as well as a wide variety of intuitive products, training, services, and literature. Call Aura Imaging Systems for a location in your area.

Aura Imaging Systems/Progen Company
International Headquarters
319 Spruce Street Redwood City, CA 94063
Tel: (800) 321-AURA (650) 367-0369 Fax (650) 261-0193
also see our Web Site at http://www.auraphoto.com
Call for the nearest location where you can have your aura photo taken. Aura cameras are located in most of the United States and in 35 countries around the globe. Information is also available about hosting an aura camera at your store or event, or purchasing an aura camera.

Manufacturer's Service Centers:
USA. Progen Co.-Aura Imaging, 319 Spruce St.,
Rewood City, CA 94063. Tel: 1 (800) 321-2872

CANADA. 365 Deguire Blvd., #814,
St. Laurent, Quebec H4N2T8. Tel: (514) 338-1466

JAPAN. Top Harajuku #2 Bldg., Rm. 204, 5-15-1 Jingumae,
Shibuya-Ku, Tokyo. Tel: (81) 3 5466 0308

EUROPE. Aura Imaging Systems, Markgrafenstr. 81,
79115 Freiburg (Germany) Tel/Fax: (49) 761 482102

AUSTRALIA. Box 592, Gold Coast Mail Ctr., QLD 4217
Tel: (61) 75 275195

HONGKONG. Unit D-E, 9/F CNT-Tower, 338 Hennessey Rd.,
Wanchai, Hong Kong. Tel: (85) 2574 0477, 2803 5097
Fax: (85) 2834 3271

SINGAPORE. 11 N. Bridge Rd., #05-61/62 Peninsula Plaza
Tel: (65) 339-0008

Clairvoyant/Psychic Readings

Jennifer Baltz offers clairvoyant aura readings on a variety of topics—including relationships, career, life transitions, departed loved ones, and your psychic gifts. She is a clairvoyant, teacher, spiritual midwife, and energy worker. Jennifer teaches basic energy awareness techniques, one-on-one and in group classes. For more information about readings by phone or in person, upcoming classes, intuitive development tapes, her newsletter, or spiritual pilgrimages, call 1 (800) 600-3404 or anonyme@aol.com.

Janice Dye is a certified Reiki practitioner and Intuitive counselor, and her work and spiritual interests have kept her busy and creative in Toronto, ON, Canada for the past 7 years. Recently, she has expanded her energy to encompass the global community of Internet Cyberspace and is available for readings through e-mail at mayasweb@idirect.com. Her home on the net is the Innerspace Station, a spiritual and metaphysical resource and growing community hub. http://web.idirect.com/~innerspa.

Barbara Martin offers personal consultations and teaches classes on a variety of metaphysical topics. She is located in Southern California. Call her for more information at: (818) 353-1977.

Dayle Schear specializes in psychometry: the art of holding objects to see the past, present, and future. She has solved missing persons and murder cases with local police departments and has appeared on many national television and radio shows. Her books are *The Psychic Within, Dare To Be Different,* and *Tarot For Beginners.* Offices in Hawaii and Lake Tahoe, Nevada. For private consultations, call: (702) 588-3337.

Psychic Investigator/Researcher

C. E. Lindgren, provides scientific research on all fields of psychic phenomena, arcane societies, Rosicrucianism, and occult topics. He has seven university degrees and 25 years of experience. As a university professor of parapsychology and medieval history, he also teaches independent courses in PSI investigation and consults with clients worldwide concerning all areas of psychic happening. Rev. Lindgren, DLitt, DEd (c) may be reached at paschal@panola.com or pboltonl@sunset.backbone.olemiss.edu. Tel: (601) 563-8954. <http://panola.com/ancients>

REFERENCES

1—WE ARE MADE OF LIGHT —
Brennan, Barbara Ann. *Hands of Light.* Bantam, New York, 1987.
Ehrmann, Max, "Desiderata," 1692.
Holland, Carlisle, D. O. "Perceptual Transference," unpublished
    medical paper.

2—WHAT YOUR AURA LOOKS LIKE —
Allan, Gina. Interview by C. E. Lindgren, 1996.
(BPI) The Berkeley Psychic Institute, Berkeley, CA. Est. 1973.
    "Meditation I and II," Clairvoyant Training Program (attended
    1989).
Brennan, Barbara Ann. *Hands of Light.* Bantam, New York, 1987.
Cayce, Edgar. "Auras," A.R.E. Press, Virginia Beach, VA, 1945.
Chopra, Deepak. *Creating Affluence: Wealth Consciousness in the
    Field of All Possibilities.* Amber-Allen Publishing/New World
    Library: San Rafael, CA, 1993.
Foundation for Inner Peace. *A Course in Miracles.* San Rafael, CA.
Hunt, Valerie. *Infinite Mind: The Science of Human Vibrations.*
    Malibu Publications, Malibu, CA, 1989.
Moss, Thelma. *The Probability of the Impossible.* J.P. Tarcher, Los
    Angeles, CA, 1974.
Payne, Buryl. *The Body Magnetic.* Psychophysics Press, 4264 Topsail,
    Soquel, CA.
Redfield, James. *The Celestine Prophecy.* Warner Books, 1993, p 42.
Schear, Dayle. Story retold from a draft, 1996. [Also appeared on the
    NBC television special *Ancient Prophecies.*]

3—SCIENCE MEETS THE UNKNOWN —
Alesandra, Patrick. *Seeing Auras.* A. Priori. (aprioripa@aol.com)
Bagnall, Oscar. *The Origin and Properties of the Human Aura.*
    University Books, NY, 1970.

Dye, Janice, Reiki Practitioner. Interview by C. E. Lindgren, 1996.

Ferguson, Sibyl. Preface to *The Aura,* by Walter Kilner. Weiser, NY, 1973.

Kilner, Walter J. *The Aura.* Weiser, NY, 1973.

Kilner, Walter J. *The Human Aura.* University Books, NY, 1965.

Krippner, S. and D. Rubin. *Galaxies of Life.* Gordon & Breach, NY, 1972.

Shepard, Leslie. "Foreword." *The Human Aura*, by Walter Kilner. University Books, NY, 1965.

4—WHERE TECHNOLOGY AND ENERGY MEET —

Brennan, Barbara Ann. *Hands of Light.* Bantam, NY, 1987.

Coggins, Guy. Interview by Susana Madden, 1996.

Hunt, Valerie. *Infinite Mind: The Science of Human Vibrations.* Malibu Publications, Malibu, CA. 1989.

Julien, Lois. Interview by Jennifer Baltz. 1996.

Liles, George. "Color me loyal, open-minded, hard to manipulate," *Provincetown Banner*, 2 November 1995, p. 2.

Moss, Thelma. *The Probability of the Impossible*. J.P. Tarcher, Los Angeles, CA, 1974.

5—AURA IMAGING PHOTOGRAPHY —

Brennan, Barbara Ann. *Hands of Light.* Bantam, New York, 1987.

Coggins, Guy. Interviewed by C. E. Lindgren, 1994.

Coggins, Guy. Interviewed by Susana Madden, 1996.

Gerber, Richard. *Vibrational Medicine.* Ingram, 1st edition, 1988.

Montanari, Carlo. Quoted from letter, 1996.

Progen. *BioFeed Back Field Photography*, 1990, video production. [1 (800) 321-AURA]

Tolan, Mary, "Let your light shine on through," *Arizona Daily Sun*, 30 April 1995.

6—THE COLORS IN YOUR AURA —

Cayce, Edgar. "Auras," A.R.E. Press, Virginia Beach, VA, 1945.

Church of Aesclepion, classes, lectures, and demonstrations.

Dye, Janice, Reiki Practitioner. Interviewed by C. E. Lindgren, 1996.

Fisslinger, Johannes. *Aura Imaging Photography.* Trans. from German by Daniela Rommel-Hathaway. Sum Press, Iowa, 1994.

Sun, Howard and Dorothy. *Color Your Life.* Bantam Books, NY, 1993.
Zukav, Gary. *The Dancing Wu Li Masters.* Quill/Morrow, NY, 1979.

8—CRYSTALS AND THE AURA —

Gardner, Joy. *Color and Crystals.* The Crossing Press, 1988.
Morse, Andrine. Unpublished manuscript, 1996.

9—LOVE COLORS —

Dye, Janice, Reiki Practitioner. Interview by C. E. Lindgren, 1996.

10—PLAYING WITH COLORS —

Baltz, Jennifer. "Harmonizing Your Life With Feng Shui." *Heart Dance Magazine*, October 1995.
Roland Hunt. *The Seven Keys to Colour Wisdom.* The C. W. Daniel Company, Ltd, England, 1940, p. 17.

11—CHAKRAS: WHEELS OF COLOR AND LIGHT —

(BPI) Berkeley Psychic Institute, Berkeley, CA. Est. 1973. "Meditation I and II," Clairvoyant Training Program (attended 1989).
Brennan, Barbara. Evening Workshop, San Francisco, CA, January 1995.
Cameron, Julia. *The Artist's Way.* G.P. Putnam's Sons, NY, 1992.
Church of Divine Man, collected oral teachings.
Morgan, Marlo. *Mutant Message Down Under.* Morgan, 1991.
Parvarandeh, Ostad Hadi. Interview, *SECRA News*, April/May 1996.
Redfield, James. *The Celestine Prophecy.* Warner Books, 1993, p 42.

12—ENERGY AWARENESS GAMES —

(BPI) Berkeley Psychic Institute, Santa Rosa, Healing I class, 1995. [As taught by Diane Zumer.]
Carroll, Lewis. *Alice's Adventures in Wonderland.* Warner Books, NY, p. 5. [original publ. date 1865]
Smith, Penelope. Interview by Jennifer Baltz, June 1996.

13—AURIC EXPERIENCES AND EXPERIMENTS —

Aljadin, spiritual practitioner of Chinese spiritual arts. Interview by C. E. Lindgren, 1996.

Beltz, Carol. Interview by C. E. Lindgren, 1996.
Brennan, Barbara Ann. *Hands of Light*. Bantam, New York, 1987.
Bruce, Catherine Hilderbrand Curran. Interview by C. E. Lindgren, 1996.
Dye, Janice. Reiki Practitioner. Interview by C. E. Lindgren, 1996.
Goodin, Charles C. Interview by C. E. Lindgren. 1996.
Heringa, Regiena. Interview by C. E. Lindgren, 1996.
Jupiter. Interview by C. E. Lindgren, 1996.

14—HOW TO SENSE THE AURA —
Allan, Gina. Interview by C. E. Lindgren, 1996.
(BPI) Berkeley Psychic Institute, Berkeley, CA. Est. 1973. "Meditation I and II," Clairvoyant Training Program (attended 1989).
(BPI) Berkeley Psychic Institute, Santa Rosa Healing I class, 1995.
Cayce, Edgar. "Auras," A.R.E. Press, Virginia Beach, VA 1945.
Redfield, James. *The Celestine Prophecy*. Warner Books, 1993, p. 44.

15—AURIC PERCEPTIONS —
Hunt, Valerie. *Infinite Mind: The Science of Human Vibrations*. Malibu Publications, Malibu, CA. 1989, p. 51.

16—CLEARING THE AURIC FIELD —
Andrews, Lynn. Interview by Sirona Knight, published in *Heart Dance Magazine*, October 1995.
(BPI) Berkeley Psychic Institute, Santa Rosa, Healing I class, 1989.

17—RESOURCES FOR PERSONAL GROWTH —
Carroll, Lewis. *Alice's Adventures in Wonderland*. Warner Books, NY, p. 54. [original publ. date 1865]

CONTRIBUTORS

Contributing Editors:

Jennifer Baltz is an intuitive teacher, writer, and clairvoyant consultant with clients worldwide. She enjoys exploring new frontiers, especially communication, spiritual energy work, and travel to sacred sites. She began her path as a spiritual teacher at the Berkeley Psychic Institute, where she became an accredited clairvoyant and teacher. She is also a Christian minister. Her hobbies include organic gardening and interspecies telepathic communication. She lives in Northern California.

C. E. Lindgren, *FCP, EdS, DLitt, DEd (cand)*, is an ordained priest, and an Adjunct Professor of Parapsychology, Metagogics, and Medieval History at universities in the US, Canada, and UK. Prof. Lindgren has written six books and over 150 journal and magazine articles. He is also a Fellow of the Royal Society of Arts, Royal Asiatic Society, College of Preceptors in England, and Master Herbologist. His upcoming works include *Spiritual Alchemists: Rosicrucians, the Brotherhood of Light* and *Spirits of the Afterlife*.

Contributors:

Blythe Arakawa works with many psychics, writers, researchers, and artists worldwide. Born & raised in Hawaii, he splits his time between Lake Tahoe and Hawaii. According to Blythe, "I feel one of my purposes in life is to help network people together."

Guy Coggins, noted inventor and technological researcher, has numerous inventions to his credit including Aura Imaging Camera 6000, mobility aids for the blind and handicapped, Second Vision (an interactive video aura camera), WinAura software, and the Living Aura. Besides his research, Mr. Coggins is president of Progen/Aura Imaging Company which specializes in high voltage power supplies, aura imaging cameras, computer imaging, and ion systems.

Ruby K. Corder, a Christian consultant, serves as executive secretary of Educational Consultants of Oxford, Inc. and lay worker for the Rose Cloister Interfaith Outreach Service. She currently lives in North Mississippi.

Janice Dye is a certified Reiki practitioner and Intuitive counselor, and her work and spiritual interests have kept her busy and creative in Toronto, ON, Canada for the past 7 years. Recently, she has expanded her energy to encompass the global community of Internet Cyberspace.

Susana Madden is a freelance writer, and photographer who has traveled extensively throughout the U.S., Canada, and Asia to holistic expos and events photographing auras.

Barbara Martin is a metaphysical teacher, psychic counselor, and writer. She is considered an international aura expert and lectures on the subject. Barbara lives in Glendale, California. Playing With Color is excerpted from her upcoming book, *Change Your Aura, Change Your Life*.

Buryl Payne, MS, PhD is a Phi Beta Kappa graduate of the University of Washington and holds advanced degrees in psychology and physics. His research work includes designing and patenting GSR type biofeedback technology, as sold by Radio Shack and Thought Technology. A former faculty member of Goddard College and Boston University, he currently designs magnetic field devices in Santa Cruz, California.